Roadmap to Analyzing a Text:

Poems, Drama, Films, Novels, Music and Dance

By

Dr. Padmore E. Agbemabiese

ISBN: 978-81-934055-3-6

First Edition: 2017
Rs. 200/-

RP
www.rochakpublishing.com

Rochak Publishing
HIG 45 Kaushambi Kunj, Kalindipuram
Allahabad - 211011 (U.P.) India
http://www.cyberwit.net
Tel: +(91) 9415091004 +(91) (532) 2552257
E-mail: info@cyberwit.net

Printed at Repro India Limited.

Roadmap to

Analyzing a Text:

Poems, Drama, Films, Novels, Music and Dance

Introduction

Anybody can write an appreciation of a text, but not everybody can write a critical analysis of a text. In every school and college, students are asked to write literary analysis essays because this type of assignment encourages the student to think about **how and why** a poem, music, short story, novel, or play was written or told. That is discovering what prompted the composition and the end goal of the text (poem, play, music, etc.).

The goal of this book is to discuss how to write the specific type of literature paper often referred to as a "critical analysis" or "interpretive analysis" of literature. This type of paper is different from merely analyzing or examining literature using the elements of literature. It is also different from an interpretive or argumentative description of a literary work. *To analyze* means "to break into parts and examine the components." *To interpret* means "to offer possible meanings." The phrase "close reading" also is sometimes used to describe this kind of writing, as it requires close examination—detailed, careful reading sentence by sentence—of one or several small parts, sometimes as little as a line (in poetry), a paragraph (in short stories and essays, or a page or two (in books) to *critically* (thoughtfully and carefully) explain a work of literature.

In literature and the other humanity courses, to interpret or critically analyze means to break a subject (such as a segment of a work of art or, in other fields, a culture, person, or event) into its constituent parts, examine these components, and offer a meaning—or alternative meanings—about each. Usually such a paper starts with an interpretive question, such as "What is a major turning point in the work of *Macbeth*?" Other interpretive questions might, instead, be used, such as "What is the relationship of Romeo to his father," "What did the one ring symbolize to the dwarves in *Lord of the Rings*," or "How does the element of chance control the fortunes of two different male characters in *The Color Purple?"*

Writing this kind of essay, and writing it well, is never easy. The fact is that strong papers begin with good planning, and good planning begins with an understanding of the task at hand. If you do not understand the assignment or what is expected of you in the essay, how can you execute the writing properly?

When I was in college, our English teachers told us that, they wanted us to learn more about literature because they wanted the art of it to expand our minds and help us discover new ways of seeing the world. We were taught to both see a work of literature as a way to understanding the time it was written, the experiences of the people who produced it, and to find the parts of that work that speak to us in our time and place. While I was skeptical, at that time, about whether or not anyone can ever really understand a culture or a time prior to their own, I do now know that literature and art provide insights that cold hard facts do not.

Today, in my classroom, I introduce students to what is called close reading. Close reading is a challenging skill to teach precisely because we are already skillful in it. When students are initiated into the discipline of literary criticism, they can analyze texts without having to think about what specific intellectual processes are taking place inside their heads. It involves a kind of self-reflectiveness which is absolutely necessary for effective understanding of texts and their figurative meanings. At times, close reading can seem like a mysterious and arcane set of practices.

Methods of analysis discussed here have served me very well in the classroom, and I encourage more lecturers to undertake the same sort of reflective process while considering these suggested formats in order to improve upon analysis and interpretation of texts among our students in our institutions.

To

Teachers and Students of the Arts.

"Every child is an artist. The problem is how to remain
an artist once he grows up."

\- Pablo Picasso

"A painter should begin every canvas with a wash of black,
because all things in nature are dark except
where exposed by the light."

\- Leonardo da Vinci

Contents

Chapter One
What is Literature?

In the attempt to define the term 'literature', one can distinguish between two general directions: a **broad** and a **narrow** definition of literature. The broad definition incorporates everything that has been written down in some form or another, i.e., all the written manifestations of a culture (hence, there are terms such as 'research literature', 'the literature on civil rights', etc.). Needless to say that such a broad definition is problematic as it does not really facilitate communication about the topic. Furthermore, this concept neglects the fact that in many cultures in the past and for a number of indigenous peoples today, literature has not been captured in written media but has been passed down in a long oral tradition of storytelling, myths, music, ritual speeches, etc. Attempts to come up with a narrow definition have, however, led to such a diversity of approaches that one can hardly talk about 'the' narrow definition. Nevertheless, it is possible to sift out some of the criteria scholars have applied in order to demarcate 'literary texts' from 'non-literary texts'. These criteria include:

1. Fictionality
2. Specialized language
3. Lack of pragmatic function
4. Ambiguity.

Fictionality

One characteristic feature of literary texts arguably is their fictionality. People usually agree that literary texts, even if they attempt to represent reality in some form or another, are ultimately products of a writer's imagination and that at least the characters and their conversations are fictitious. Thus, some of the characters in Sir Walter Scott's **historical novels** for example, are pure inventions although they are situated in authentic historical contexts, and they have fictitious conversations with historical figures, that actually existed. On the other hand, texts that are normally read as non-fiction, like a reportage, often display features that remind one of literature. Consider the following example:

Sesca Rompas climbed on to a plastic stool and peered through a dirty window at her brother, Aldo Kansil, lying motionless in a bed below.

He was a pitiful sight: two drips attached, arms swathed in bandages, his face an angry mosaic of burns...

Taken out of its context, it is difficult to decide what type of text this is. If one looks at the way this passage is written, one can easily imagine this to be the beginning of a novel. First, it is a descriptive passage which introduces a certain **setting**: The window is dirty and so high up that the woman needs a plastic stool to be able to peep through it. The brother's desolate state is captured in epithets describing his motionless, afflicted body. Secondly, characters are introduced and a mini **plot** is elaborated: A woman called Sesca Rompas visits her brother, Aldo Kansil, who is in hospital. Just like the beginnings of novels, this text passage is written in such a way as to urge the reader to read on and to find out more, e.g., who are these people, why is the brother in hospital, what happened? Moreover, the language used is reminiscent of literary texts. We can identify **rhetorical devices** such as **alliteration** ("bed below"), **metaphor** ("angry mosaic of burns"), **asyndeton** and **ellipsis** ("two drips attached, arms swathed in bandages [...]"). In other words: the text uses embellishments to present a specific 'story-world' and to attract the reader's attention. And yet, these are, in fact, the opening lines of a newspaper article (*The Independent*, 16 October 2002) which deals with the victims of a Balinese bomb attack. With this information in mind, we suddenly stop regarding this text as fiction: We take it for granted that the people described here are real and that the events related in the text are also real.

What does this example tell us? First of all, we can say that the boundaries between 'fact' and 'fiction' are often blurred and by no means always identifiable. More importantly, whether a text is fictional or not, is perhaps less the consequence of some inherent quality of the text but of a reader's attitude towards it. If I know the text above is from a newspaper I automatically assume that the 'story' must be real. By contrast, if this had been the beginning of a novel, I would undoubtedly have classified these characters and the setting as fictitious. In other words: We as readers are conditioned through education and cultural norms to approach texts in certain ways. In this view, fictionality is no longer an inherent feature of literary texts but part of our expectations of what a literary text should be like. Likewise, literary language is partly determined by the fact that we want to read it as 'literary'. This will be explored in the following section.

Specialized Language

People often say that literary language is 'special' and that it differs considerably from normal everyday language. The linguist Roman Jakobson spoke of the **poetic function** of literary texts in his essay "Linguistics and Poetics: Closing Statement" (1960), i.e., the fact that literary texts draw attention to the language they employ. As the Russian Formalists maintained in the early twentieth century, literary texts make use of language in such a way that it becomes strange and unfamiliar in a given context. They called this process **de-familiarization**. The following example from Charles Dickens' novel *Bleak House* illustrates this process:

> Foot passengers, jostling one another's umbrellas, in a general infection of ill-temper, and losing their foot-hold at street-corners, where tens of thousands of other foot passengers have been slipping and sliding since the day broke (if this day ever broke), adding new deposits to the crust upon crust of mud, sticking at those points tenaciously to the pavement, and accumulating at compound interest.
>
> (Dickens, *Bleak House*, ch. 1)

The way the bad November weather in London is described here has hardly anything to do with the way people would normally talk about the weather. One thing is particularly conspicuous: the blending of a description of natural phenomena ("mud", bad weather) with the jargon of the world of finance ("deposits", "accumulating", "compound interest"). By combining these two areas, the words are taken out of their usual context and put into another one, which thus becomes 'new' and 'unfamiliar' to the reader. We are attracted by this strange linguistic description and we start to wonder why such language is used here. One explanation might be that London as one of the financial centers in the mid-nineteenth century has become so immersed in its business that even nature participates in it and is no longer 'natural'.

One area where the 'literariness' of language seems to be particularly obvious is poetry. Poetry is often marked by a conspicuous shape (lines, stanzas, etc.), a dense structure (thematically and linguistically), specific **prosodic features** and **rhetorical devices**. Now, as the example above from *The Independent* shows, even non-literary texts frequently use rhetorical devices and certain patterns to arouse the readers' interest. Still, we do not necessarily classify them as literature. We do not, for example, consider a telephone directory a literary text although it is indeed extremely structured and ordered in a special way. Nor do we regard the above-mentioned newspaper article a poem, for example. And yet, is this really because the language in this article does not qualify for poetry or because we are simply not used to looking at newspaper articles in such a way? Consider the following sentence from the same article:

Just around the corner, an anxious-looking couple were standing close together, clutching plastic bags.

At first sight, this looks like a 'normal' sentence. There is nothing conspicuous about the words or the sentence structure. What happens if one pays attention to the rhythm of this sentence and displays it accordingly?

Just around the corner,
An anxious-looking couple
Were standing close together,
Clutching plastic bags.

All of a sudden, one realizes that the sentence actually follows a regular metrical pattern, namely a **trimeter** with alternating stressed and unstressed syllables. Does that make the sentence poetic? Again, one can see that the line between literary and non-literary language is a very fine one and that the decision whether a text is literary or not largely depends on the way we look at the text and perceive its language. A lot of contemporary poetry plays with our alleged 'knowledge' of the literariness of texts. Have a look at the following "Found Poem" by Ronald Gross:

All too often, humans who sit and stand
Pay the price of vertical posture. Sitting
And standing combine with the force of gravity,
Exerting extra pressure on veins and tissues
In and around the rectal area.
Painful, burning hemorrhoids result.
The first thought of many sufferers
Is to relieve their pain and their discomfort.
Products, however, often used for this
Contain no anesthetic drug at all, or one
Too weak to give the needed pain relief,
Or only lubricate. But now, at last
There is a formulation which provides
Pain-killing power, prolonged relief, on contact.

(Gross, *Open Poetry*)

Although this text must originally have been an advert for anti-hemorrhoids medication, we can now read its language as literary language and thus perceive the text as a piece of literature simply because it has been transformed by means of formalization and rearrangement. Trained readers of literature may even identify this text as a **sonnet** because it follows the structural convention of fourteen lines with an **octave** and a **sestet** (here presented as two tercets). What this example also shows is that the way we read texts depends very much on the context in which we read them. If we had read this text on an information leaflet we would never have dreamed of looking at it as poetry and paying closer attention to its language. As soon as it appears in the guise of a sonnet, however, our reading practice also changes and we can start treating it as 'literary', e.g., by attempting an interpretation. This leads us to the next criterion often mentioned in discussions of literary texts, namely their lack of a pragmatic function.

Lack of Pragmatic Function

Undoubtedly, texts derive their meaning partly from their context. I read a novel as a novel because it is presented in a certain way (bound, with a title on the front page, sometimes the word 'novel' in the subtitle, and a plot summary as well as commentary on the back cover). Moreover, I use the novel as a novel and not as a cookery book, a newspaper or an encyclopedia of garden plants, for example. Why is that? One might argue that these texts, in contrast to literary texts, have a definite **pragmatic function**, i.e., they are written and used for a specific purpose, e.g., to assist with the cooking or gardening or, generally, to inform the reader. A piece of literary writing, on the other hand, need not have been intended by the author for any specific purpose. It sometimes seems as though literature was just written into time and space, to nobody in particular and without any function.

Nevertheless, it would be a mistake to take that as a basic rule. Even literary texts do have a purpose, e.g., to criticize, to educate or even just to entertain. The fact that authors like Salman Rushdie, for example, are persecuted by political and religious groups shows that something must be attributed to their writings which other people consider dangerous or at least influential in some way or another. While non-literary texts may have a more clearly defined and generally agreed-upon function, literary texts can have a range of purposes which again depend on the reader. Thus, I can read a book simply to have a good laugh or, for that matter, a good cry, or I draw analogies with my own life and try to gain consolation or advice from the text. The text as such may not necessarily tell me how I have to use it but the reading practices I have been taught in school, at university, etc. will certainly influence my approach to texts. In other words: Even if we claim that a literary text has no immediate pragmatic function, we usually start to ascribe one to it in our usage or treatment of that text. While non-literary texts seem to have an inherent pragmatic function, i.e., they were 'born' to be a telephone book, a time-table, a women's magazine, etc., literary texts gain their more specific and possibly individual pragmatic function in the reading process.

Ambiguity

People generally accept the view that literary texts are far more ambiguous and thus often more complicated than non-literary texts. If one reads a recipe, for example, or a time-table or an instruction manual, the meaning expressed in these texts is presumed to be more or less fixed and not open to interpretation. In fact, these texts must not be open to interpretation because then they just would not 'work'. A time-table has to be precise in order for people to be able to rely on it. And then people using the same recipe for carrot cake should reach approximately the same result by following the step-by-step instructions.

This is certainly not the case if ten people read a novel, for example. As classroom discussions show, different students can come up with rather different interpretations of what a specific literary text 'means' or what it tries to convey. This is also reflected in the vast amount of divergent critical interpretations of literary texts published over the years. So what is it that makes literary texts so ambiguous? For one thing, there is obviously the 'human factor': When we read a text we usually bring to bear on it certain expectations and interests, and inevitably we start looking for exactly those things that seem relevant to us. Thus, for example, Christina Rossetti's long poem *Goblin Market* can be interpreted as a simple fairytale, a poem restating the biblical concepts of sin and redemption, or indeed as a combination of all of these facets at the same time. Or the poem *The Weaver Bird* by Kofi Awoonor, which is a postcolonial poem that utilizes the symbol of the weaver bird to represent the coming of the colonialists to Africa, but could easily be misconstrued due to the language and imageries used. No matter which interpretation one favors, one can find evidence for all of them in the text if one only searches through it thoroughly. This example illustrates that literary texts indeed must have some quality which makes them more 'open' than non-literary texts. One can say that literary texts always express meaning on different levels or in different layers. In other words: They express something beyond their literal 'meaning', and these other layers of meaning can be explored by attentive reading and analysis. It is a bit like archaeology: the deeper one digs the more interesting one's findings are likely to be. At the same time, one needs suitable equipment for 'digging out' hidden meanings. That is where literary analysis becomes important and where the fun begins once one has mastered the tools essential to analysis and interpretation.

Chapter Two

What Is Literary Analysis

What is often referred to as literary analysis involves reading of poems, stories, plays, novels, and essays, and thinking about them, discussing them, and writing about them in a candid manner. In this way, literary analysis involves the four processes of reading, thinking, discussing, and writing, and its practical pedagogical value lies in its tendency to stimulate these activities and thereby improving the reader's ability to perform them. Unknown to us, careful reading increases the reader's vocabulary and general verbal sensitivity and sophistication.

A consistent reading and analyzing of texts can lead the reader to think critically about what has been read beyond the surface meaning. Discussions of the text with friends, in and out of the classroom, also sharpen reading and thinking skills and increase the reader's ability to express thoughts in oral contexts and in writing. In this way, literary analysis becomes a process that stimulates the reader's desire to organize and record thoughts excellently in writing and in speaking. Thus, the study of literature can be seen as a practical intellectual discipline. In many ways, it directly involves the reader in the analysis of difficult literary texts, and in doing so it develops verbal skills which are transferable to other contexts in life. Over the years, I have come to believe that a person trained in the study of literature is better equipped than most to read, comprehend, and analyze other kinds of texts (newspapers, reports, poems, music, plays, human behavior etc.). This makes the case for why in many situations, for example, English majors make such highly qualified candidates for law school.

I will also make the case that literary study pays dividends far beyond the obvious resulting from increased verbal ability. Indeed, reading literature increases knowledge in an active, intellectually challenging way that other more passive activities, such as watching television cannot do. A thorough grounding in literature automatically provides knowledge of our literary heritage while at the same time increasing the reader's awareness of cultural values, history, sociology, psychology, and almost every branch of human knowledge.

Beyond all these values of literary analysis, I can convincingly say it expands our capacity to sympathize with other human beings, enhances our ability to see and imagine human complexity, and broadens our intellectual horizons by enlarging our power to experience life vicariously. It develops our skills for discerning aesthetic principles and deepens our ability to take pleasure in the written word. Indeed, we live in an age that grossly and dangerously underestimates the power and importance of the imagination.

A Word for Teachers of Literary Analysis

Literary analysis is a vital stage in the development of students' critical thinking skills. Bloom's Taxonomy illustrates that analysis should come at the fourth level, right after comprehension and application. What this means is that students must be able to understand and describe the text before they are able to analyze its elements.

Teaching literary analysis is often a daunting and overwhelming task. After all, it is essentially guiding students slowly through the process of critical thinking and understanding literature. That's not a simple undertaking. Most importantly, with so many ways to go about doing it, where do we begin?

To guide students toward discovering literature all on their own, the steps of this process need to be introduced in a simplified form. It's very important for the student to understand that literary analysis is indeed a *process* where there is no right or wrong answer. This empowers students to be passionate about their topics and, most importantly, encourages them to look beyond the words on the page.

My method of teaching literary analysis is one of demystification that attempts to make the practice as transparent as possible. In brief terms, it boils literary analysis down into three simple, discrete steps: *(a) Understanding*, *(b) Noticing*, and *(c) Explaining*.

The Process to literary analysis

1. **Choose a Topic**

Some students need guidance when choosing a topic, but others have ideas that they would like to explore. Topics can be divided into the main literary elements:

a. Characters

b. Themes

c. Literary devices

d. Setting

e. The Narrative.

2. Focus the Topic

Here is where many students will need to do a lot of brainstorming, outlining, and specific thinking about the element on which they would like to focus.

a. The brainstorming process involves mapping out the different aspects of the chosen element.

b. Make a choice by narrowing down the selection and focusing the ideas.

c. Come up with a question to answer (thesis statement): What do you want to explore about the topic? Why does it stand out to you?

d. Answer the "why" question. Instead of letting students simply describe the text, "why" pushes them to analyze and even synthesize.

This aspect is vital to student understanding, as most of the time a teacher is able to identify a relevant thesis related to modern-day issues and concepts. Here is where real-world application, analysis, and synthesis can begin to form in this piece of writing.

3. Gather Textual Evidence

Collecting material to answer or support your question is often a time-consuming stage, because most of the close reading will occur here. It's important for students to know that they're allowed to research the topic or text before starting to write. Many students feel that they should not be using Google or Wikipedia to research their texts. Here is where the teacher can have an honest discussion about digital citizenship, and how to tell credible academic sources from non-credible ones.

Show students that close reading and gathering evidence doesn't have to be a mundane, one-dimensional task.

- **a. Identify** common themes, repetitions, and patterns.
- **b. Categorize** elements, tone, and narrative style.
- **c. Highlight** characterization, setting, and foreshadowing.
- **d. Label** character types, symbols, and metaphors.

4. Introduce, Evidence, Analyze

Learning through writing and literary analysis happens through stages (read Bloom's Taxonomy far below). At this stage of writing, students have already accomplished remembering, understanding, and applying. Next comes analysis:

Introduce

Students should introduce their point in one or two clear topic sentences. Next, it's important to provide evidence that supports the main topic in order to convince the reader of the stated point of view. There are a few ways students can add their evidence.

Evidence: This can be done through three ways

a. Quotation: When providing evidence word for word from a primary or secondary source, students should be reminded to use quotation marks only if the words have not been altered.

b. Summary: Students summarize a piece of evidence by restating it in a shorter form using their own words.

c. Paraphrase: Students explain a piece of evidence using their own words.

At this stage, it's important to use the lesson as a reminder to cite and give credit for words and ideas that belong to others. A conversation with the class about academic honesty is very important to help them understand intellectual property. This conversation will also prepare them for honesty and ethics in the real or academic world.

Analyze

This critical stage is often a learning curve for many students. It's important that the teacher helps them distinguish between descriptive writing and analytical writing. **Descriptive writing** answers the "who," "what," "where," and "how" questions. It often tends to summarize the text. **Analytical writing**, however, answers to the "why" question. When students consider the question, "Why is this point important?", it pushes them beyond mere description into ideas that are convincing, argumentative, and defend a position.

5. Conclusion

A strong conclusion outlines not only the main ideas of the essay, but it also works to provide a solution to a real-life problem. Students can focus on concluding with what they hope to get out of their analysis (what they have learned), or provide closure to the topic. Most importantly, students should seize the conclusion as an opportunity to provide their own opinion and reflection about their process of analyzing the text. The self-reflection here would be a vital key for teachers to assess the writing process and a great opportunity to provide essential feedback to the student.

Bloom's Taxonomy at a Glance

Bloom's taxonomy offers a perfect way to learn and write about a text. Here is a brief explanation and guide to the main categories of the Taxonomy of Educational Objectives (*Handbook One*, pp. 201-207):

a. **Knowledge** "involves the recall of specifics and universals, the recall of methods and processes, or the recall of a pattern, structure, or setting."

b. **Comprehension** "refers to a type of understanding or apprehension such that the individual knows what is being communicated and can make use of the material or idea being communicated without necessarily relating it to other material or seeing its fullest implications."

c. **Application** refers to the "use of abstractions in particular and concrete situations."

d. **Analysis** represents the "breakdown of a communication into its constituent elements or parts such that the relative hierarchy of ideas is made clear and/or the relations between ideas expressed are made explicit."

e. **Synthesis** involves the "putting together of elements and parts so as to form a whole."

f. **Evaluation** engenders "judgments about the value of material and methods for given purposes." (Source: https://cft.vanderbilt.edu/guides-sub-pages/blooms-taxonomy/)

Overview of the Process of Literary Analysis

The goal of writing a literary analysis is to systematically take apart and look at some important or interesting segment of a literary work. To do so, you should choose an important turning point, or a scene, character, activity, or some other segment of a literary work, break it into parts, and analyze it part by part. You can examine each part thoroughly using the elements of literature to help explain its meanings, compare/contrast each part to others in the literary work, or apply a literary theory or other point of view to each part.

The structure you use is that of a logical, balanced essay, with a brief introduction, a series of body sections explaining each part, and a brief conclusion. If your instructor suggests or allows it, you also may have a *brief* first body section, after the introduction, which summarizes the main elements of the work (if your instructor is unacquainted with it) or reports biographical, historical, or other background.

In your introduction and conclusion and throughout the body paragraphs of your paper, you should consistently quote and paraphrase the literary work that is your subject as you analyze parts and their possible meanings. These quotations and paraphrases help you support what you are saying by showing clearly just what the author of the work has written.

If you are writing a research paper, you also must add quotations, paraphrases, or other references from additional sources—whether other literary works, professional critics, or other interpretive resources—using these additional resources to add more analysis and interpretation. You also will need a full MLA bibliography/Works Cited page.

How do you organize this type of paper?

A critical analysis may take on the same form as a basic description of the elements, moving through all the main elements from simplest to most complex, offering interpretation of each in turn.

However, a more complex version is to organize by selecting specific parts, places, or examples from a work. In this type of organizing, you choose the parts that help you answer your initial research question. In writing the paper, you start with the initial question; then you order the series by the order of simplest to most abstract, by the parts in the work, by their importance, or, sometimes, by some other development that makes sense. You might do so by their order of presentation in the work, by their order of importance or interest, or by an order of unfolding or development (e.g., from most obvious to least, or from simplest to most complex).

The conclusion you reach in such a paper is your own. However, you use balanced, factual gathering of evidence from the work you have chosen and—in a research paper—from other sources to support your interpretation.

Chapter Three

Writing a Literary Analysis Paper

The Purpose of a Literary Analysis:

A literary analysis is not merely a summary of a literary work. Instead, it is an argument about the work that expresses a writer's personal perspective, interpretation, judgment, or critical evaluation of the work. This is accomplished by examining the literary devices, word choices, or writing structures the author uses within the work. The purpose of a literary analysis is to demonstrate why the author used specific ideas, word choices, or writing structures to convey his or her message.

How to Approach Literary Analysis

1. Read the text closely several times. Focus on the ideas that are being presented. Think about the characters' development and the author's writing technique. What might be considered interesting, unusual, or important?

2. Brainstorm a list of potential topics. Highlight important passages in the text and take notes on these passages. Later, when writing the paper, these notes should help a writer to remember which aspects of the story caught his/her attention. The topic chosen should always be based on a writer's interpretation of the author's message. Here are some things a writer may want to consider when brainstorming for a literary analysis.

a) Character: What observations might a writer make about the characters? Are there discrepancies in what they think, say, or do? Are the observations a writer makes different from what other characters say? How does the author describe the characters? Are the characters "dynamic" (a dynamic character is a character that undergoes important changes throughout the work)? Are the characters "static" characters (a static character is a character that stays the same throughout the work)? Are the characters "flat" characters (a flat character is a character that does not have vivid character traits) or "round" characters (a round character is a character that has vivid character traits)? Are the characters symbolic or representative of some universal quality? Is it possible that two characters in the text might be compared or contrasted?

b) Setting: Is there a relationship between the work's setting and its mood? Does the setting reflect the work's theme? How does the setting impact the characters? Does a change in the setting affect the mood, characters, or conflict?

c) Plot: How might the beginning of the work be interpreted? How does the plot build suspense? Does the author use techniques such as foreshadowing or flashback? Are there patterns of cause-effect relationships? Do events occur in a logical order? Examine the events that lead to the climax and determine how the work ends?

d) Theme: What is the major idea or theme of the work? How does the author relay this theme? Is there a greater meaning to the details given? How do the characters' moods affect the theme? What allusions are made throughout the work? Are there repeating patterns or symbols? What does the title say about the theme?

e) Dialogue: What is the purpose of the dialogue? Is the dialogue appropriate in terms of word choice or sentence length? How does the dialogue impact the characterization? How does the author use the dialogue to show the mood of the characters? How does this aid the author's message? How does the dialogue impact the plot?

f) Imagery: In what way might a specific image or series of images be analyzed? How might the development of images throughout the work be explained? Are the images important to the meaning of the work? How are images interrelated with other literary elements?

g) Figures of speech: How are figures of speech such as similes, metaphors, and hyperboles used throughout the text? How are these figures of speech important in relation to the meaning of the text? Are figures of speech interrelated between other literary elements?

h) Tone: How might describe the attitude of the author or the tone of the work be described? Is the tone serious, playful, casual, formal, or somber? How does the author achieve this tone? How does the tone impact the author's message? Does the author say one thing but mean another? Does the author take the subject seriously or treat it lightly?

i) Rhyme/Rhythm: Do the author's words, sentences, or paragraphs seem to share a similar rhyme pattern? What type of rhythm does the author seem to be creating? How is this rhyme/rhythm impacting the author's message? Does the author use the different rhymes/rhythms as a sound device for the literary work? How does the author do this?

j) Point of View: What point of view do the characters display? First, second, or third? How does this point of view affect the theme, plot, or conflict of the work? How might the author's point of view impact a writer's analysis? Might the character's first-person point of view draw a writer to feel as though he/she is hearing a personal account and cause him/her to feel an intimate connection with the character? Might the author's third person account cause a writer to feel as if the author is acting as the narrator of the story? Or might it cause a writer to believe that the narrator is an omniscient being who is distant but knows the character's thoughts and feelings?

3. Think about what the author is trying to say. Why is this important? When viewing this work as a piece of art, what might a writer's response be? What might a writer's reactions be to the ideas presented in the work? Are these ideas truthful or relevant to today and how? If a writer were asked what they thought of this work how might they respond? What points might a writer make?"

4. Select a topic that has sufficient supporting evidence. A writer should make sure to include specific details to support the topic. Use highlighted sections of the book as evidence to support the topic that has been chosen.

5. Write a working thesis. The analysis will need a strong thesis that states a writer's perspective but also allows it to be debated. The thesis should state a writer's opinion, but it should also allow readers to arrive at their own conclusions.

Example of a **debatable thesis**:

Pride and Prejudice is about Elizabeth Bennet's effort to overcome her own proud behavior and discrimination towards Mr. Darcy, as well as how her family is affected by the haughtiness and preconceptions of the society around them.

(*This is a debatable thesis because it asks the reader, "Does Elizabeth actually exhibit haughtiness and preconceptions? Is this why she doesn't get along with Mr. Darcy? How is Elizabeth's family affected by the haughtiness and preconceptions of the society around them?"*)

Avoid a **non-debatable thesis**:

Example: *Pride and Prejudice* is about five sisters and their journey to find love.

(*This thesis is non-debatable because it is undisputable. The paper is framed as a summary rather than as a literary analysis.*)

6. Make an extended list of evidence. Find more evidence from the text to support the working thesis. Then select the evidence that will be used in the paper.

7. Refine the thesis. Make sure the thesis fits with the evidence that has been presented.

8. Organize the evidence. Match the evidence to the order of the thesis. Delete any of the original textual supports that may no longer follow the thesis, and gather new evidence if needed.

9. Interpret the evidence. When writing a literary analysis, it is very important for writers to make sure they express their own personal interpretation of the work. Be careful that the literary analysis is not a summary.

10. Create a rough draft. When writing a rough draft, there are several methods that may aid a writer in creating a strong final draft. Here are a few methods:

a) Outline: An outline will help a writer to organize his/her thoughts and ideas. It will remind a writer of the order of the thesis, as well as the supporting points he/she would like each topic sentence to have.

b) Free-write: A short, ten minute free-write will help to get all of a writer's thoughts on paper. It will allow a writer to focus on the content, rather than the punctuation and spelling. Once the free-write is complete, a writer can read through it and circle the points that are strong, as well as omit the ones that are not.

c) Bubble Map: A bubble map will allow a writer to draw connections from one idea to the next. It will give a writer a visual idea of the direction of the literary analysis, as well as help a writer to see the connections between the topics. This can help a writer transition from one topic to another more fluidly.

11. Revise the Analysis. After completing the first draft, revise the analysis by considering the following questions:

A. Is the thesis clearly stated in the first paragraph?

B. Is the sentence structure varied?

C. Does the structure of the analysis emphasize the main ideas?

D. Is the third-person point of view used throughout the entire essay?

E. Has the present tense been used to discuss the work and past tense to describe the author's background?

A. Have quotation marks been used around direct quotations?

B. Have the sources been cited correctly according to MLA style?

C. Has extraneous information that does not support the thesis been eliminated?

D. Have clear transitions been used between sentences and paragraphs?

12. Proofread. Once the content of the essay is well-developed, it should be proofread for grammar, punctuation, and spelling. It is often helpful to read the paper slowly and clearly out loud. If possible, another person should listen and read along as the paper is being read.

The paper should be printed and proofread several times until an accurate final copy is created. Be alert to common grammatical errors such as sentence fragments, comma splices, or run-on sentences. Remember to consult a style manual for grammatical or citation questions, and if further assistance is desired, group workshops and individual appointments are available free of charge through Tutoring Services

(Source: www.tc.umn.edu/~jewel001/CollegeWriting/WRITELIT/LitAnalysis/default.htm)

Chapter Four

Guide to Analysis of Poetry, Music, Fiction and Drama

This is a guide to what you might look for in analyzing literary texts, particularly poetry, drama, film, music and fiction. An analysis explains what a work of literature means, and how it means it; it is essentially an articulation of and a defense of an interpretation which shows how the resources of literature are used to create the meaningfulness of the text. Before undertaking any analysis of a text, note that everything as a text has a pre-text, subtext, context, inter-textuality and point of view.

i. Text could be a novel, drama, poetry, music, film, the way you dress or talk, in fact, the way you look.

ii. Pre-text is something that happened before the text was written. It is what leads the author to act or write a poem, a song, a piece of drama etc. Writers use it to get to a conversation.

iii. Subtext is what is used to mask the real issue being discussed in the text. An example is how African Americans used the Negro spirituals to hide their escape to the north. Another example is George Orwell's *Animal Farm* which was used to address the revolution of France.

iv. Content of something such as a speech, piece of writing, website, or television program is the information it gives, or the ideas or opinion expressed in it.

v. Inter-textuality is what other external works or texts the writer involves to explore his or her subject. It could be another text or music used to advance an argument.

vi. Context is the position from which a writer is coming from—political, social, economic, spiritual, point of view, position, or status. Every text is set (setting) in a historical, social, political etc. accuracy.

vii. Point of View is the person whom the author uses to tell his story. Hence, we see or hear the story from a narrator. This could be the First Person Point of View or the Third Person Point of view. Each has its limitations and advantages. Remember, someone is always between the reader and the action of the story. That someone is telling the story from his or her own point of view. This angle of vision, the point of view from which the people, events, and details of a story are viewed, is important to consider when reading a story.

There are people who resist analysis, believing that it 'tears apart' a work of art; however, a work of art is an artifice, that is, it is made by someone with an end in view: as a "made" thing, it can be and should be analyzed as well as appreciated. There are several main reasons for analyzing literature:

1. The ultimate end of analysis is, first and foremost, a deeper understanding and a fuller appreciation of the literature — you learn to see more, to uncover or create richer, denser, more interesting meanings. I have a brief page on the ideas of depth, complexity and quality as they relate to literature.

2. Secondly, as literature uses language, images, the essential processes of meaning-making, analysis can lead to a more astute and powerful use of the tools of meaning on the reader's part.

3. Thirdly, analysis should also teach us to be aware of the cultural delineations of a work, its ideological aspects. Art is not eternal and timeless but is situated historically, socially, intellectually, written and read at particular times, with particular intents, under particular historical conditions, with particular cultural, personal, gender, racial, class and other perspectives. Through art we can see ideology in operation. This can be of particular use in understanding our own culture and time, but has historical applications as well. See my brief page on ideology for an expansion of this.

4. A fourth function of analysis is to help us, through close reading and through reflection, understand the way ideas and feelings are talked

about in our culture or in other times and cultures — to have a sense both of communities of meaning, and of the different kinds of understanding there can be about matters of importance to human life. Art can give us access to the symbolic worlds of communities: not only to the kinds of ideas they have about life, but also to the way they feel about them, to the ways they imagine them, to the ways they relate them to other aspects of their lives.

Understanding the Author's Purpose and Perspective in a Text

Authors do not write in vacuum. Each piece of writing has a purpose and a goal. The concept of **author's purpose** is an idea that is often discussed in academic circles, and identifying the author's purpose is central to understanding a text.

Author's Purpose: Reasons for Writing

Any text that you encounter (whether the menu from your favorite restaurant or Shakespeare's *Macbeth*) serves an intended purpose for the writer. These include providing education, information, entertainment, and persuasion or mobilization. These purposes can have variables or other aspects to them.

1. Writing to Entertain

One primary purpose of texts that are written to entertain is to amuse readers. This does not mean that the text must be happy; the text could be a tragedy, but the main reason for writing the text is to amuse readers.

Examples of Texts that Are Written to Entertain:

1. Stories/novels
2. Poems
3. Dramas
4. Songs

Of course, this is not to say that stories, poems, songs or plays cannot be informative and educative. These texts may even express values and ideas that will persuade readers to view the world differently. Nonetheless, if the text is not entertaining, readers are unlikely to find enlightenment or be moved by such a text. Therefore, one of the purposes of any text, poem, song and play is to entertain readers.

2. Writing to Inform

Another purpose of texts is that they are written to inform so as to enlighten the reader or provide the reader with information about a topic.

Examples of Texts That Are Written to Inform

1. Expository Essays or Articles
2. Instructions or Directions
3. Encyclopedias or Other Reference Texts

Again, the lines separating these distinctions may blur. A text that is written to inform may educate as well as entertain readers. For example, many readers find reading the newspaper to be very entertaining, but the primary purpose of the majority of the text is to provide information. From other reference texts, some readers may learn about the Liberty Tower, flying saucers, dinosaurs, or robots solely for enjoyment, but the author's main purpose in writing such texts is to inform or educate the reader.

3. Writing to Persuade

In a text that is written to persuade, the author's primary purpose is to compel readers to take action, convince them of an idea through argument, or to reaffirm their existing beliefs.

Examples of Texts That Are Written to Persuade

1. Advertisements
2. Campaign Speeches
3. Persuasive Letters or Notes

As with other purposes for writing, there may be crossover with writing to persuade. For example, readers may find a television commercial video to be extremely entertaining. Such a video may even go viral because so many people find it enjoyable. Nonetheless, the primary purpose of such a text is to persuade people to purchase the product or service.

To discover an author's primary purpose in a text, when you want to analyze the text, follow the guidelines below:

GENRE	AUTHOR'S PURPOSE	MAIN IDEA OF THE OF THE TEXT	AUTHOR'S PERSPECTIVE
What kind of text is this? a. Drama b. Novel c. Poetry d. Article e. Music f. Etc.	**Why did the author write this piece?** a. To educate b. To inform c. To entertain d. To persuade e. To explain, Expose, Mobilize	What is the central or the most important idea in the text?	a. What does the author think about the main or central idea in the text? b. What is the author's attitude towards this main idea c. How does the author treat the main idea?
	Give **supporting evidence** from the text to support which purpose you indicate		Give **supporting evidence** from the text to prove that what you say the author thinks is really true.

NOTE: As you begin your analysis and interpretation, pay attention to cues and clues left in the text by the author:

1. The presence of metaphors, symbols, and imageries in a literary text influences and improves the quality of thematic and the aesthetic appreciation of the text. This is crucial to analysis and interpretation.

2. Identifying the linguistic metaphors or features in the text provides access to the underlying conceptual and hidden meanings of the text (literal and figurative meanings) and opens up new ways to interpretation and analysis of the text, thereby making the text more appealing.

3. There are also independent factors, such as social expectations that influence interpretation of a text thematically and aesthetically.

4. Pay attention to how poetic techniques are employed by the author in the text. The recognition of metaphorical meaning structures and other devices in the text lead to improved judgments or interpretation or analysis of the text.

5. Look for the socio-political pressure (social expectations) and other factors (cultural, religion, culture etc.) that play a crucial role in the creation of the text.

Selected Guidelines for Writing a Literary Critical Analysis

What is a literary critical analysis?

A literary critical analysis explains a work of fiction, poetry or drama by means of interpretations. The goal of a literary analysis (as with any other analysis) is to broaden and deepen your understanding of a work of literature.

What is an interpretation?

An interpretation is an individual response that addresses meaning. Example: The mother in Jamaica Kinkaid's story "Girl" cannot speak directly of her love for her daughter, so Kinkaid uses details about a woman's everyday life to convey her pride and anxiety about her daughter.

How do you develop an interpretation?

Interpretations are developed by an in-depth examination of a text. An interpretation often will be the thesis of your paper.

How do you conduct an "in-depth" examination of a text?

1. Before reading the work, make sure to examine the title carefully. Often the title is a clue to an important idea in the work.

2. Make sure you look up in the dictionary any words with which you are not familiar.

3. After reading the work the first time, ask yourself the following questions:

a) What is the geographical, historical and social setting? How does this affect the story or poem?

b) Who is (are) the main character(s)?

c) Who are the secondary characters, and how are they linked to the main characters?

d) Does the main character change? If so, how and why? If not, why not?

e) What is the conflict? Can you trace the development and resolution of the conflict?

f) Who is telling the story? How does this influence the story or poem?

g) In poetry, can you find a pattern of rime and meter?

4. As you re-read the work, make sure you can answer these questions. Then ask yourself the following questions, which may help you to discover deeper meanings that will lead you to an interpretation.

a) Can you summarize the author's meaning in one paragraph?

b) Can you state a theme of the work in one sentence?

c) Can you identify any symbols or metaphors? What do they mean?

How do you prove your interpretation?

You prove your interpretation by finding a pattern of examples in the literature that support your idea. You find this pattern in the literary elements, such as plot, point of view, character, setting, symbols, tone, and style. In poetry, the uses of language (rime, meter and metaphors) are also patterns that can support your interpretation.

If interpretations are an individual response, are all interpretations valid?

Because an interpretation must be supported, the strength or weakness of your interpretation rests on the strength or weakness of your argument. In other words, you must organize a discussion that convinces the reader that your point of view is astute.

Where do you find evidence to support your interpretation?

In a literary analysis evidence is found mainly from the work you are discussing. Secondary sources (published critical analyses) may support your point of view as well.

How much of the story should you retell in a critical analysis?

You do need to locate your reader to the scene or section of the poem that you are discussing; therefore, some plot summary is necessary, but re-telling the story or a poem is not considered an analysis. You can assume your reader has read the work.

What should be documented in a critical analysis?

Any secondary sources must, of course, be documented. Also, direct quotes should be documented. Unlike secondary sources, a summary of a literary scene or event does not need documentation. Typically, MLA style documentation is used.

Chapter Five
Critical Analysis of Poetry

The process of analyzing a poem

The elements of analysis discussed below are designed to help you identify the ways in which poetry makes its meaning, especially its 'parts'; they do not give a sense of how one *goes about* analyzing a poem. It is difficult to give a prescription, as different poems call on different aspects of poetry, different ways of reading, different relationships between feeling, images and meanings, and so forth. My general advice, however, is this:

1. Look at the title

2. Read the poem for the major indicators of its meaning — what aspects of setting, of topic, of voice (the person who is speaking) seem to dominate, to direct your reading?

3. Read the ending of the poem — decide where it 'gets to'

4. Divide the poem into parts: try to understand what the organization is, how the poem proceeds, and what elements or principles guide this organization (is there a reversal, a climax, a sequence of some kind, sets of oppositions?)

5. Pay attention to the tone of the poem — in brief, its attitude to its subject, as that is revealed in intonation, nuance, the kind of words used, and so forth.

6. Now that you've looked at the title, the major indicators of 'topic', the ending, the organization, the tone, read the poem out loud, trying to project its meaning in your reading. As you gradually get a sense of how this poem is going, what its point and drift is, start noticing

more about how the various elements of the poetry work to create its meaning. This may be as different as the kind of imagery used, or the way it uses oppositions, or the level of realism or symbolism of its use of the natural world.

Reading poetry well is a balance among and conjunction of qualities: experience, attention, engagement with the qualities which make the poem resonant or compelling, close reading of structure and relationships. It's an acquired talent, you have to learn it. When you do, however, more and more meaning, power and beauty start leaping out at you.

Elements of analysis

Here then are some questions to apply to your analysis in order to see how the poem is making its meaning: they cover genre, the speaker, the subject, the structure, setting, imagery, key statements, the sound of the poetry, language use, intertextuality, the way the reader is formed by the poem, the poem's historical placement, and ideology or 'world-view'

1. What is the genre, or form, of the poem?

Is it a sonnet, an elegy, a lyric, a narrative, a dramatic monologue, an epistle, an epic etc.? Different forms or genres have different subjects, aims, conventions and attributes. A love sonnet, for instance, is going to talk about different aspects of human experience in different ways with different emphases than is a political satire, and our recognition of these attributes of form or genre is part of the meaning of the poem.

2. Who is speaking in the poem?

Please remember that if the voice of the poem says "I", that doesn't mean it is the author who is speaking: it is a voice in the poem which speaks. The voice can be *un-dramatized* (it's just a voice, it doesn't identify itself), or *dramatized* (the voice says "I", or the voice is clearly that of a particular persona, a dramatized character).

Identify the voice. What does the voice have to do with what is happening in the poem, what is its attitude, what is the tone of the voice (tone can be viewed as an expression of attitude)? How involved in the action or reflection of the poem is the voice? What is the perspective or 'point of view' of the speaker? The perspective can be social, intellectual, political, even physical — there are many different perspectives, but they all contribute to the voice's point of view, which point of view affects how the world of the poem is seen, and how we respond.

3. What is the argument, thesis, or subject of the poem?

What, that is to say, is it apparently 'about'? Start with the basic situation, and move to consider any key statements; any obvious or less obvious conflicts, tensions, ambiguities; key relationships, especially conflicts, parallels, contrasts; any climaxes or problems posed or solved (or not solved); the poem's tone; the historical, social, and emotional setting.

4. What is the structure of the poem?

There are two basic kinds of structure, formal and thematic.

Formal structure is the way the poem goes together in terms of its component parts: if there are parts —stanzas, paragraphs or such — then there will be a relation between the parts (for instance the first stanza may give the past, the second the present, the third the future).

Thematic structure, known in respect to fiction as 'plot', is the way the argument or presentation of the material of the poem is developed. For instance, a poem might state a problem in eight lines, an answer to the problem in the next six; of the eight lines stating the problem, four might provide a concrete example, four a reflection on what the example implies. There may well be very close relations between formal and thematic structure. When looking at thematic structure, you might look for conflicts, ambiguities and uncertainties, the tensions in the poem, as these give clear guides to the direction of meanings in the poem, the poem's 'in-tensions'.

5. How does the poem make use of setting?

There is the setting in terms of time and place, and there is the setting in terms of the physical world described in the poem.

In terms of the physical world of the poem, setting can be used for a variety of purposes. A tree might be described in specific detail, a concrete, specific, tree; or it might be used in a more tonal way, to create mood or associations, with say the wind blowing mournfully through the willows; or it might be used as a motif, the tree that reminds me of Kathryn, or of my youthful dreams; or it might be used symbolically, as for instance an image of organic life; or it might be used allegorically, as a representation of the cross of Christ (allegory ties an image or event to a specific interpretation, a doctrine or idea; symbols refer to broader, more generalized meanings).

Consider this as a spectrum, from specific, concrete, to abstract, allegorical: concrete — tonal -connotative — symbolic — allegorical

6. How does the poem use imagery?

"Imagery" refers to any sort of image, and there are two basic kinds. One is the images of the physical setting, described above. The other kind is images as figures of speech, such as metaphors. These figures of speech extend the imaginative range, the complexity and comprehensibility of the subject. They can be very brief, a word or two, a glistening fragment of insight, a chance connection sparked into a blaze (warming or destroying) of understanding; or they can be extended analogies, such as Donne's 'conceits' or Milton's epic similes.

7. Are there key statements or conflicts in the poem that appear to be central to its meaning?

Is the poem direct or indirect in making its meanings? If there are no key statements, are there key or central symbol, repetitions, actions, motifs (recurring images), or the like?

8. How does the sound of the poetry contribute to its meaning?

Pope remarked that "the sound must seem an echo to the sense": both the rhythm and the sound of the words themselves (individually and as they fit together) contribute to the meaning.

9. Examine the use of language.

What kinds of words are used? How much and to what ends does the poet rely on connotation, or the associations that words have (as "stallion" connotes a certain kind of horse with certain sorts of uses)? Does the poem use puns, double meanings, ambiguities of meaning?

10. Can you see any ways in which the poem refers to, uses or relies on previous writing?

This is known as *allusion* or *intertextuality*. When U-2's Bono writes "I was thirsty and you kissed my lips" in "Trip Through Your Wires," the meaning of the line is vastly extended if you know that this is a reference to Matthew 25:35 in the Bible, where Jesus says to the saved in explanation of what they did right, "I was thirsty and you wet my lips."

11. What qualities does the poem evoke in the reader?

What sorts of learning, experience, taste and interest would the 'ideal' or 'good' reader of this poem have? What can this tell you about what the poem 'means' or is about? The idea is that any work of art calls forth certain qualities of response, taste, experience, value, from the reader, and in a sense 'forms' the reader of that particular work. This happens through the subject matter, the style, the way the story is told or the scene set, the language, the images, the allusions, all the ways in which we are called by the text to construct meaning. The theorist Wayne Booth calls the reader as evoked or formed by the text the "implied reader."

12. What is your historical and cultural distance from the poem?

What can you say about the difference between your culture's (and sub-culture's) views of the world, your own experiences, on the one hand, and those of the voice, characters, and world of the poem on the other? What is it that you might have to understand better in order to experience the poem the way someone of the same time, class, gender and race might have understood it? Is it possible that your reading might be different from theirs because of your particular social (race, gender, class, etc.) and historical context? What about your world governs the way you see the world of the text? What might this work tell us about the world of its making?

13. What is the world-view and the ideology of the poem?

What are the basic ideas about the world that are expressed? What areas of human experience are seen as important, and what is valuable about them? What areas of human experience or classes of person are ignored or denigrated? A poem about love, for instance, might implicitly or explicitly suggest that individual happiness is the most important thing in the world, and that it can be gained principally through one intimate sexually-based relationship — to the exclusion, say, of problems of social or political injustice, human brokenness and pain, or other demands on us as humans. It might also suggest that the world is a dangerous, uncertain place in which the only sure ground of meaningfulness is to be found in human relationships, or it might suggest on the other hand that human love is grounded in divine love, and in the orderliness and the value of the natural world with all its beauties. What aspects of the human condition are foregrounded, what are suppressed, in the claims that the poem makes by virtue of its inclusions and exclusions, certainties and uncertainties, and depictions of the way the natural and the human world is and works? For a brief elaboration of the concept of ideology, see my page on the subject.

Chapter Six

An Approach to Analyzing Fiction

The analysis of fiction has many similarities to the analysis of poetry. As a rule, a work of fiction is a narrative, with characters, with a setting, told by a narrator, with some claims to represent 'the world' in some fashion. The topics in this section are plot, character, setting, the narrator, figurative language, the way reality is represented, the world-view.

1. Plot.

As a narrative a work of fiction has a certain arrangement of events which are taken to have a relation to one another. This arrangement of events to some end — for instance to create significance, raise the level of generality, extend or complicate the meaning — is known as 'plot'. Narrative is integral to human experience; we use it constantly to make sense out of our experience, to remember and relate events and significance, and to establish the basic patterns of behavior of our lives. If there is no apparent relation of events in a story our options are either to declare it to be poorly written or to assume that the lack of relation is thematic, mean to represent the chaotic nature of human experience, a failure in a character's experience or personality, or the lack of meaningful order in the universe.

In order to establish significance in narrative there will often be coincidence, parallel or contrasting episodes, repetitions of various sorts, including the repetition of challenges, crises, conciliations, episodes, symbols, motifs. The relationship of events in order to create significance is known as the plot.

2. Character.

Characters in a work of fiction are generally designed to open up or explore certain aspects of human experience. Characters often depict particular traits of human nature; they may represent only one or two traits — a greedy old man who has forgotten how to care about others, for instance, or they may represent very complex conflicts, values and emotions. Usually there will be contrasting or parallel characters, and usually there will be significant to the selection of kinds of characters and to their relation to each other. As in the use of setting, in fact, in almost any representation in art, the significance of a character can vary from the particular, the dramatization of a unique individual, to the most general and symbolic, for instance the representation of a "Christ figure" or the deity "*Nyigbla*" among the Anlo Ewes.

3. Setting.

Narrative requires a setting; this as in poetry may vary from the concrete to the general. Often setting will have particular culturally coded significance — a sea-shore has significance for us different from that of a dirty street corner, for instance, and different situations and significances can be constructed through its use. Settings, like characters, can be used in contrasting and comparative ways to add significance, can be repeated, repeated with variations, and so forth.

4. The Narrator.

A narration requires a narrator, someone (or more than one) who tells the story. This person or persons will see things from a certain perspective, or *point of view*, in terms of their relation to the events and in terms of their attitude(s) towards the events and characters. A narrator may be external, outside the story, telling it with an ostensibly objective and omniscient voice; or a narrator may be a character (or characters) within the story, telling the story in the first person (either central characters or observer characters, bit players looking in on the scene). First-person characters may be *reliable*, telling the truth, seeing things right, or they may be *unreliable*, lacking in perspective or self-knowledge. If a narration by an omniscient external narrator carries us into the thoughts of a character in the story, that character is known as a *reflector character*: such a character does not know he or she is a character, is unaware of the narration or the narrator. An omniscient, external narrator may achieve the narrative by telling or by showing, and she may keep the reader in a relation of *suspense* to the story (we know no more than the characters) or in a relation of *irony* (we know things the characters are unaware of).

In any case, who it is who tells the story, from what perspective, with what sense of distance or closeness, with what possibilities of knowledge, and with what interest, are key issues in the making of meaning in narrative. For a fuller discussion, see my page Narrative point of view: some considerations.

5. Figurative language.

As in poetry, there will be figurative language; as in drama, this language tends to be used to characterize the sensibility and understanding of characters as well as to establish thematic and tonal continuities and significance.

6. Representation of reality.

Fiction generally claims to represent 'reality' (this is known as representation or *mimesis*) in some way; however, because any narrative is presented through the symbols and codes of human meaning and communication systems, fiction cannot represent reality directly, and different narratives and forms of narrative represent different aspects of reality, and represent reality in different ways. A narrative might be very concrete and adhere closely to time and place, representing every-day events; on the other hand, it may for instance represent psychological or moral or spiritual aspects through symbols, characters used representatively or symbolically, improbable events, and other devices. In addition, you should remember that all narrative requires selection, and therefore it requires exclusion as well, and it requires devices to put the selected elements of experience in meaningful relation to each other (and here we are back to key elements such as coincidence, parallels and opposites, repetitions).

6. World-view.

As narrative represents experience in some way and as it uses cultural codes and language to do so, it inevitably must be read, as poetry, for its structure of values, for its understanding of the world, or world-view, and for its ideological assumptions, what is assumed to be natural and proper. Every narrative communication makes claims, often implicitly, about the nature of the world as the narrator and his or her cultural traditions understand it to be. The kind of writing we call "literature" tends to use cultural codes and to use the structuring devices of narrative with a high degree of intentionality in order to offer a complex understanding of the world. The astute reader of fiction will be aware of the shape of the world that the fiction projects, the structure of values that underlie the fiction (what the fiction explicitly claims and what it implicitly claims through its codes and its ideological understandings); will be aware of the distances and similarities between the world of the fiction and the world that the reader inhabits; and will be aware of the significances of the selections and exclusions of the narrative in representing human experience.

III: Analysis of Prose in Fiction

Someone is always speaking in a novel, whether it is a narrator who is not a character within the fiction, or a character within the narrative—the persona. Consequently, both the particular ideas, attitudes, feelings, perspectives of that speaker, and the concerns and attitudes of the novel as a whole, will be presented through the prose. The analytical reader needs to understand what information is conveyed and how it is conveyed. The following is a guide to some things to look for, and contains:

A. prose: the language; sentence structure; imagery and setting; discourse features.

B. characterization

C. genre and tradition

A. The Passage as Prose.

1. The language:

1. What kind of language is used? Here are some possibilities:

Is the language:

1. abstract or concrete language
2. language of emotions or of reason
3. language of control or language of openness

2. What are the connotations of the language? How much language is connotative? What areas of experience, feeling, and meaning are evoked? When Conrad writes that a gate was "a neglected gap," we have to take notice, as a gate is not ordinarily a gap, nor is the issue of neglect or care usually applied to gaps. Conrad intends to imply, to connote, certain qualities through his language use.

3. How forceful is the language? (See also imagery and sentence structure)?

4. What aspects of feeling are supported or created by the sound of the language?

a. by the vowel and consonant sounds — soft or hard long or short

b. by how the words go together — e.g. smoothly, eliding, so that one slides into the other, or separated by your need to move your mouth position.

2. Sentence structure: Meaning is created by how the sentences sound, by how they are balanced, by the force created by punctuation as well as by language:

a. by the stresses on words, and the rhythm of the sentence

b. by the length of the sentence

c. by whether the sentence has repetitions, parallels, balances and so forth

d. by the punctuation, and how it makes the sentence sound and flow.

3. Imagery and setting: Images and use of setting can tell you a great deal about a character, a narrator, a fictional work:

a. Imagery as figurative language: what sort of metaphors, similes and analogies did the speaker use, and what does that tells you about their outlook and sensibility?

b. Images as motifs: are they recurring images? What ideas or feelings are aroused by them, what people or events are brought to mind by them?

c. Imagery as setting: How is the setting used? To create a sense of realism? To create mood? To represent or create a sense of states of mind or feelings? To stand for other things (i.e. symbolic or allegorical — as for instance *Wuthering Heights*. Thrushcroft Grange in *Wuthering Heights* might be said to stand for two ways of viewing the world or two different sociological perspectives, and jungle in *Heart of Darkness* might be said to stand for the primeval past or for the heart of humankind)?

4. Discourse features

a. How long does the person speak?

b. Are the sentences logically joined or disjointed, rational or otherwise ordered, or disorderly?

c. What tone or attitude does the talk seem to have?

d. Does the speaker avoid saying things, deliberately or unconsciously withhold information, and communicate by indirection?

e. To what extent and to what end does the speaker use rhetorical devices such as irony?

B. Characterization: The idea here is that the various features of the prose, above, will support features of characterization which we can discuss in somewhat different terms.

1. What ideas are expressed in the passage, and what do they tell you about the speaker?

2. What feelings does the speaker express? What does that tell you about them? Are their feelings consistent?

3. Does the character belong to a particular character type or represent a certain idea, value, quality or attitude?

4. What is the social status of the character, and how can you tell from how they speak and what they speak about?

5. What is the sensibility of the speaker? Is the person ironic, witty, alert to the good or attuned to evil in others, optimistic or pessimistic, romantic or not romantic (cynical, or realistic?).

6. What is the orientation of the person — how aware are they of their own and others' needs, and of their environments?

7. How much control over and awareness of her emotions, her thoughts, her language does the speaker have?

8. How does the narrator characterize the character through comment or through description?

C. Genre & Tradition

Different traditions and genres tend to use language, characters, setting and plot differently, and this may show in individual passages. Is it a satire, a comedy, a tragedy, a romance? Is it a novel of social comment, an exploration of an idea? (There are more kinds.) Is it in a certain sub-genre like a detective novel, science fiction, etc.? Is it an allegory or a satire, is it realistic or more symbolic? How does this genre, sub-genre or tradition tend to use setting, characters, language, mood or tone? Does this one fit in?

IV: Writing an Analytical Essay

Your purpose in writing an analytical essay is to convey your sense of what the text is saying, and how the text creates its meaning — the use of the various aspects and devices mentioned in the previous sections. The simplest way to open your essay is with a statement of what you have decided the meaning of the text, the most sufficient interpretation, is. The body of your essay is then a presentation or 'defense' of your interpretation: you demonstrate the ways in which the text makes the meaning you believe it to have. In the conclusion you sum up your findings or recapitulate your argument briefly, and extend the significance of your reading if you wish — this is where you comment on the more general, cultural or moral or technical significances of the theme and techniques of the text. You may begin you essay in other ways — by stating what the main barriers are to an interpretation of the poem or what the main difficulties with arriving at an interpretation are, for instance, and how consequently you intend to deal with the text, or by stating what sorts of options you have in terms of emphases and why you have chosen the one(s) you have chosen. It is important to give the reader a sense of *how* you are proceeding in the essay and *why*.

There is no sure-fire formula for essay writing. The form your essay takes will likely vary with the nature of your evidence (quotations from the text, principally, or from other sources), with your sense of how the text is structured and shaped, with your interpretation, and with your sense of what issues are most relevant. Obviously, you will have to make some organizational decisions. In writing on a poem, for example, do you go through a poem stanza by stanza showing how the meaning is developed? If this is your method, be sure you avoid the pitfalls: mere paraphrase, providing an unselective running commentary, and disorganization of kinds of evidence. An alternative approach might focus on the poem aspect by aspect (the point of view, the voice, the setting, and so forth). The pitfalls here are not being able show how the various aspects tie together to create meaning, and assuming that each aspect deserves equal and exhaustive treatment. Fiction is usually analyzed by considering one or more aspects of the work in the categories of theme (ideas, meanings), and/or of fictional techniques (plot, point of view, etc.).

Remember that there are different kinds of literature in each genre, and that different kinds may rely on different devices. A poem may be narrative; it may be a dramatic monologue; it may be a collection of images with no human in sight; it may develop a logical argument; it may work allusively, analogically, symbolically and so forth; it may have a careful stanza-by stanza development, or it may depend on repetitions, images, and so forth. A work of fiction might be allegorical, it might use magical realism, it might concentrate on the effects of the environment, or it might attempt metaphorically to represent the interior lives of characters. Figure out what the main devices and strategies are, and concentrate on them, adding the lesser ones later and not necessarily in full. Try, if you are not sure of your interpretation, starting with the simplest, most obvious situation — two lovers are meeting, say — and add other possible points of meaning as they seem to extend or illuminate the dramatic situation — for instance a storm is threatening, the meeting is seen from only one lover's point of view, each stanza gives a different meaning to what the significance of physical love might be, and so forth. Always deal with the 'form' as well as the 'content', however, with how the way something is said shapes what it means. Write what you have to say as clearly and precisely as you can. Have someone proof-read your paper for you for spelling and grammatical errors and for intelligibility.

(Adapted from Lye, John. "John Lye's Course and Source Page" *Critical Reading: A Guide*. 2008.)

Chapter Seven

How to Analyze Drama

The word, "Drama" comes from Greek word meaning action, play, or deed. This meaning carries forward to our modern usage as it bears the connotation of a story to be acted out. Dramas revolve around conflict or contrasts of character. The plays that you have the option of researching, though from separate time periods, are rich in symbolism and metaphors and often social commentary by the playwright.**Structure of Drama**

Dramatic structure is the plot structure of a dramatic work such as a play or screenplay. Many scholars have analyzed dramatic structure, beginning with Aristotle in his Poetics. According to Freytag, a drama is divided into five parts, or acts, which some refer to as a **dramatic arc**:

1. Exposition,
2. Rising Action,
3. Climax,
4. Falling Action, and
5. Dénouement/Resolution,

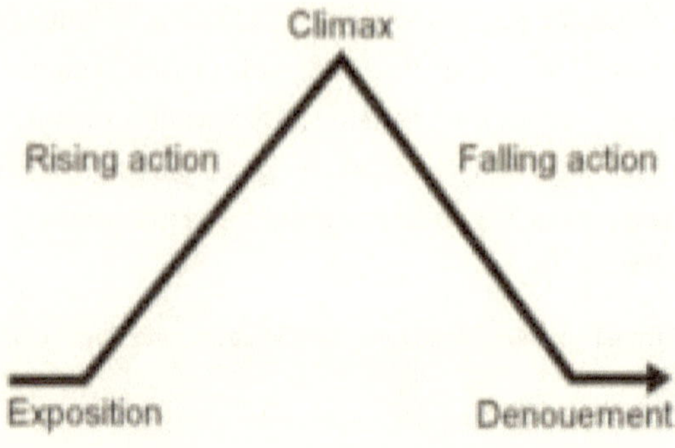

The visual representation above is Freytag's analysis of dramatic structure. It is called Freytag's Pyramid. It is also known as a plot mountain.

1. Exposition (plot device): The exposition provides the background information needed to properly understand the story, such as the protagonist, the antagonist, the basic conflict, and the setting. The exposition ends with the inciting moment, which is the incident that without there would be no story. The inciting moment sets the remainder of the story in motion beginning with the second act, the rising action. The exposition often relates to the dénouement.

2. Rising action: During rising action, the basic conflict is complicated by the introduction of related secondary conflicts, including various obstacles that frustrate the protagonist's attempt to reach their goal. Secondary conflicts can include adversaries of lesser importance than the story's antagonist, who may work with the antagonist or separately, by and for themselves.

3. Climax (turning point): The third act is that of the climax, or turning point, which marks a change, for the better or the worse, in the protagonist's affairs. If the story is a comedy, things will have gone badly for the protagonist up to this point; now, the tide, so to speak, will turn, and things will begin to go well for him or her. If the story is a tragedy, the opposite state of affairs will ensue, with things going from good to bad for the protagonist.

4. Falling action: During the falling action, the conflict between the protagonist and the antagonist unravels, with the protagonist winning or losing against the antagonist. The falling action might contain a moment of final suspense, during which the final outcome of the conflict is in doubt.

5. Resolution: The comedy ends with a dénouement (a conclusion) in which the protagonist is better off than at the story's outset. The tragedy ends with a catastrophe in which the protagonist is worse off than at the beginning of the narrative.

Although Freytag's analysis of dramatic structure is based on five-act plays, it can be applied (sometimes in a modified manner) to short stories and novels as well.

To be a great actor, one must be a detective, one must always question "why do I do what I do."

a. Super objective- Characters ultimate wants.

b. Obstacles- What is in your way?

c. Tactics- How you will achieve your objective?

A great actor must also be in the moment to allow the other characters to affect him or her. It is like a partner dance in *Agbadza*, *Kinka* or *Salsa*. Both must be intimate, communicate, be sensitive to each breath, movement, etc. for it to be effortless.

Beats are extremely important. They can mean a change in blocking and emotional movement. Steady beat (hearing it, feeling it, "seeing it", and being moved to it) is important for developing sense of passion, unity and cohesion. An internalized awareness of beat coordinates actions and movements.

Text and Theatre

When one deals with dramatic texts one has to bear in mind that drama differs considerably from poetry or narrative in that it is usually written for the purpose of being performed on stage. Although plays exist which were mainly written for a reading audience, dramatic texts are generally meant to be transformed into another mode of presentation or medium: the theatre. For this reason, dramatic texts even look different compared to poetic or narrative texts. One distinguishes between the primary text, i.e., the main body of the play spoken by the characters, and secondary texts, i.e., all the texts 'surrounding' or accompanying the main text: title, dramatis personae, scene descriptions, stage directions for acting and speaking, etc. Depending on whether one reads a play or watches it on stage, one has different kinds of access to dramatic texts.

As a reader, one receives first-hand written information (if it is mentioned in the secondary text) on what the characters look like, how they act and react in certain situations, how they speak, what sort of setting forms the background to a scene, etc. However, one also has to make a cognitive effort to imagine all these features and interpret them for oneself.

While we can actually see and hear actors play certain characters on stage, we first decipher a text about them when reading a play script and then at best 'see' them in our mind's eye and 'hear' their imaginary voices. Put another way, stage performances offer a multi-sensory access to plays and they can make use of multimedia elements such as music, sound effects, lighting, stage props, etc., while reading is limited to the visual perception and thus draws upon one primary medium: the play as text. This needs to be kept in mind in discussions of dramatic texts, and the following introduction to the analysis of drama is largely based on the idea that plays are first and foremost written for the stage.

Plays have many different elements or aspects, which means that you should have lots of different options for focusing your analysis. Playwrights—writers of plays—are called "wrights" because this word means "builder." Just as shipwrights build ships, playwrights build plays. A playwright's raw materials are words, but to create a successful play, he or she must also think about the performance—about what will be happening on stage with sets, sounds, actors, etc. To put it another way: the words of a play have their meanings within a larger context—the context of the production. When you watch or read a play, think about how all of the parts work (or could work) together.

For the play itself, here are some important contexts to consider:

1. The time period in which the play was written

2. The playwright's biography and his/her other writings

3. Contemporaneous works of theater (plays written or produced by other artists at roughly the same time)

4. The language of the play
5. Setting
6. Plot
7. Themes
8. Characters

Depending on your assignment, you may want to focus on one of these elements exclusively or compare and contrast two or more of them and how they contribute to the meaning of the play. Keep in mind that any one of these elements may be more than enough for a dissertation, let alone a short reaction paper. Also remember that in most cases, your assignment will ask you to provide some kind of analysis, not simply a plot summary—so don't think that you can write a paper about *A Doll's House* that simply describes the events leading up to Nora's fateful decision.

Since a number of academic assignments ask you to pay attention to the language of the play and since it might be the most complicated thing to work with, it's worth looking at a few of the ways you might be asked to deal with it in more detail.

Response papers

Instructors in drama classes often want to know what you really think. Sometimes they'll give you very open-ended assignments, allowing you to choose your own topic; this freedom can have its advantages and disadvantages. On the one hand, you may find it easier to express yourself without the pressure of specific guidelines or restrictions. On the other hand, it can be challenging to decide what to write about. The elements and topics listed above may provide you with a jumping-off point for more open-ended assignments. Once you've identified a possible area of interest, you can ask yourself questions to further develop your ideas about it and decide whether it might make for a good paper topic.

For example, if you were especially interested in the lighting, how did the lighting make you feel? Nervous? Bored? Distracted? It's usually a good idea to be as specific as possible. You'll have a much more difficult time if you start out writing about "imagery" or "language" in a play than if you start by writing about that ridiculous face Helena made when she found out Lysander didn't love her anymore.

If you're really having trouble getting started, here's a three-point plan for responding to a piece of theater—say, a performance you recently observed.

1. Make a list of five or six specific words, images, or moments that caught your attention while you were sitting in your seat.

2. Answer one of the following questions: Did any of the words, images, or moments you listed contribute to your enjoyment or loathing of the play? Did any of them seem to add to or detract from any overall theme that the play may have had? Did any of them make you think of something completely different and wholly irrelevant to the play? If so, what connection might there be?

3. Write a few sentences about how each of the items you picked out for the second question affected you and/or the play.

This list of ideas can help you begin to develop an analysis of the performance and your own reactions to it.

Chapter Eight

Elements of Drama: A Review

Description

Role/Character: An actor's portrayal of a character in a drama, developed with attention to background, motivation, speech, and physical traits

Relationship(s): The connection(s) between people, events, or circumstances

Time and Place: The setting, time period (e.g., past, present, future), duration (e.g., one day), and sequence of the action of a story or drama

Tension: A heightened mental or emotional state resulting from uncertainty about how the conflict or problem in a drama will be resolved

Focus and Emphasis: The theme, character, problem, event, moment in time, or center of visual interest (e.g., in a tableau) that gives purpose to a drama

Elements of Drama

1. **Role/Character:** Who are the characters?

2. **Relationship(s):** What are the relationships among the characters (friends, family, strangers, and strong-weak)?

3. **Setting-Time and Place:** Where and when is this taking place?

4. **Tension:** What is happening? Why is there conflict?

5. **Focus and Emphasis:** Who or what is the focus of the scene?

6. Students' Choice of Element: Students' choice of question

Critical Analysis Process

A. Initial Reaction

What is your first impression of this tableau?

B. Description

What elements do you see in the work?

Ask the critical "describing" question for each element:

1. **Role/Character:** Who are the characters?

2. **Relationship(s):** What are the relationships between the characters?

3. **Time and Place:** When and where is this taking place?

4. **Tension:** What is happening? Why is there conflict?

5. **Focus and Emphasis:** Who or what is the focus of the scene?

C. Analysis and Interpretation

How do the actors show us/help us understand what is happening?

Ask the critical "how" question for each element:

1. **Role/Character:** How do they establish their characters (e.g., body language, facial expressions, use of props)?

2. **Relationship(s):** How do they establish their relationship with each other (e.g., eye contact, body positioning)?

3. **Time and Place:** How do they establish the time and place (e.g., use of props, costumes, furniture, blocking, areas of the stage)?

4. **Tension:** How do they convey to the audience what is happening? How do they make the conflict clear?

5. Focus and Emphasis: How do they create focus (e.g., body positioning, staging, lights, where the characters are looking)?

D. Expression of an Informed Point of View

1. How effectively does the group use and combine the elements to illustrate the scenario (i.e. What works?)?

2. Considering the elements, is there anything else the group could do to illustrate the scenario more clearly (i.e. What doesn't work and why? What might work better?)

What to consider when writing an analysis

To successfully analyze literature, you'll need to remember that authors make specific choices for particular reasons. Your essay should point out the author's choices and attempt to explain their significance. Another way to look at a literary analysis is to consider a piece of literature from your own perspective. Rather than thinking about the author's intentions, you can develop an argument based on any single term (or combination of terms) listed below. You'll just need to use the original text to defend and explain your argument to the reader.

Character - representation of a person, place, or thing performing traditionally human activities or functions in a work of fiction

- **Protagonist** - The character the story revolves around.
- **Antagonist** - A character or force that opposes the protagonist.
- **Minor character** - Often provides support and illuminates the protagonist.
- **Static character** - A character that remains the same.
- **Dynamic character** - A character that changes in some important way.
- **Characterization** - The choices an author makes to reveal a character's personality, such as appearance, actions, dialogue, and motivations.

Look for: Connections, links, and clues between and about characters. Ask yourself what the function and significance of each character is. Make this determination based upon the character's history, what the reader is told (and not told), and what other characters say about themselves and others.

Connotation - implied meaning of word. BEWARE! Connotations can change over time. Connotation is an idea or feeling that a word invokes in addition to its literal or primary meaning. Words have cultural, political, social and religious dimensions to them. E.g. "the word "discipline" has unhappy connotations of punishment and repression"

- *confidence/ arrogance*
- *mouse/ rat*
- *cautious/ scared*
- *curious/ nosey*
- *frugal/ cheap*

Denotation - dictionary definition of a word. In other words, it is the literal or primary meaning of a word, in contrast to the feelings or ideas that the word suggests. E.g. "beyond their immediate denotation, the words have a connotative power". The action or process of indicating or referring to something by means of a word, symbol, etc.

Diction - word choice that both conveys and emphasizes the meaning or theme of a poem through distinctions in sound, look, rhythm, syllable, letters, and definition

Figurative language - the use of words to express meaning beyond the literal meaning of the words themselves

*a) **Metaphor*** - contrasting to seemingly unalike things to enhance the meaning of a situation or theme without using **like** or **as**

a. *You are the sunshine of my life.*

b) ***Simile*** - contrasting to seemingly unalike things to enhance the meaning of a situation or theme using **like** or **as**

a. What happens to a dream deferred, does it dry up ***like*** *a raisin in the sun*

c) ***Hyperbole*** - exaggeration

a. I have a million things to do today.

d) ***Personification*** - giving non-human objects human characteristics

a. America has thrown her hat into the ring, and will be joining forces with the British.

Foot - grouping of stressed and unstressed syllables used in line or poem

a) ***Iamb*** - unstressed syllable followed by stressed

a. Made famous by the Shakespearian sonnet, closest to the natural rhythm of human speech

i. How ***do*** I ***love*** thee? ***Let*** me ***count*** the ***ways***

b) ***Spondee*** – stressed, stressed

a. Used to add emphasis and break up monotonous rhythm

i. Blood boil, mind-meld, well- loved

c) ***Trochee*** - stressed unstressed

a. Often used in children's rhymes and to help with memorization, gives poem a hurried feeling

i.

While I ***nod***ded, ***near***ly ***nap***ping, ***sud***den***ly*** there ***came*** a ***tap***ping,

d) ***Anapest*** – unstressed, unstressed stressed

a. Often used in longer poems or "rhymed stories"

i. 'Twas the ***night*** before ***Christ***mas and ***all*** through the ***house***

e) Dactyls - stressed unstressed, unstressed

a. Often used in classical Greek or Latin text, later revived by the Romantics, then again by the Beatles, often thought to create a heartbeat or pulse in a poem

i. ***Pic***ture your***self*** in a ***boat*** on a ***ri***ver,

With ***tan***gerine ***trees*** and mar***ma***lade skies.

The iamb stumbles through my books; trochees rush and tumble; while anapest runs like a hurrying brook; dactyls are stately and classical.

Imagery - the author's attempt to create a mental picture (or reference point) in the mind of the reader. Remember, though the most immediate forms of imagery are visual, strong and effective imagery can be used to invoke an emotional, sensational (taste, touch, smell etc.) or even physical response.

Meter - measure or structuring of rhythm in a poem

Plot - the arrangement of ideas and/or incidents that make up a story

a) Foreshadowing - When the writer clues the reader in to something that will eventually occur in the story; it may be explicit (obvious) or implied (disguised).

b) Suspense - The tension that the author uses to create a feeling of discomfort about the unknown

c) Conflict - Struggle between opposing forces.

d) Exposition - Background information regarding the setting, characters, plot.

e) Rising Action - The process the story follows as it builds to its main conflict

f) Crisis - A significant turning point in the story that determines how it must end

g) Resolution/Denouement - The way the story turns out.

Point of View - pertains to who tells the story and how it is told. The point of view of a story can sometimes indirectly establish the author's intentions.

a) Narrator - The person telling the story who may or may not be a character in the story.

b) First-person - Narrator participates in action but sometimes has limited knowledge/vision.

c) Second person - Narrator addresses the reader directly as though she is part of the story. (i.e. "You walk into your bedroom. You see clutter everywhere and...")

d) Third Person (Objective) - Narrator is unnamed/unidentified (a detached observer). Does not assume character's perspective and is not a character in the story. The narrator reports on events and lets the reader supply the meaning.

e) Omniscient - All-knowing narrator (multiple perspectives). The narrator knows what each character is thinking and feeling, not just what they are doing throughout the story. This type of narrator usually jumps around within the text, following one character for a few pages or chapters, and then switching to another character for a few pages, chapters, etc. Omniscient narrators also sometimes step out of a particular character's mind to evaluate him or her in some meaningful way.

Rhythm - often thought of as a poem's timing. Rhythm is the juxtaposition of stressed and unstressed beats in a poem, and is often used to give the reader a lens through which to move through the work. (See meter and foot)

Setting - the place or location of the action. The setting provides the historical and cultural context for characters. It often can symbolize the emotional state of characters. Example – In Poe's *The Fall of the House of Usher*, the crumbling old mansion reflects the decaying state of both the family and the narrator's mind. We also see this type of emphasis on setting in Thomas Mann's *Death in Venice*.

Speaker - the person delivering the poem. Remember, a poem does not have to have a speaker, and the speaker and the poet are not necessarily one in the same.

Structure (fiction) - The way that the writer arranges the plot of a story.

Look for: Repeated elements in action, gesture, dialogue, description, as well as shifts in direction, focus, time, place, etc.

Structure (poetry) - The pattern of organization of a poem. For example, a Shakespearean sonnet is a 14-line poem written in iambic pentameter. Because the sonnet is strictly constrained, it is considered a closed or fixed form. An open or free form poem has looser form, or perhaps one of the author's invention, but it is important to remember that these poems are not necessarily formless.

Symbolism - when an object is meant to be representative of something or an idea greater than the object itself.

a) *Cross - representative of Christ or Christianity*

b) *Bald Eagle - America or Patriotism*

c) *Owl - wisdom or knowledge*

d) *Yellow - implies cowardice or rot*

Tone - the implied attitude towards the subject of the poem. Is it hopeful, pessimistic, dreary, worried? A poet conveys tone by combining all of the elements listed above to create a precise impression on the reader.

Chapter Nine

Guidelines to Analyzing and Interpreting Film

I recently met a group of Social Studies teachers, in Accra-Ghana, who indicated that well-researched and well-crafted feature films and movies dealing with historical events are excellent ways to supplement curriculum and vary the classroom experience. I was taken in, because this means an educational presentation of such a film requires that showing the film be accompanied by a process of at least some literary analysis and a comparison with the historical record. Not only does this approach prepare students for a process that will be useful throughout their adult years or writing career, but it has obvious cross-curricular benefits. In like manner, a colleague, Professor Africanus Aveh, at the University of Ghana, Legon, recently noted to me that "Currently, film text is taught in several disciplines: English and other Modern Languages, Theatre and Media Studies, Anthropology, etc. Understanding film text is now becoming necessary in the arts and social sciences." This brings to the fore the value of film in education and the need to study how to analyze film in general.

The power of film to make an emotional connection and how best to enable people to experience this power through education, has become a theme of roundtable discussions in colleges and in the media. An experience with film enhances self-concept and develops a sense of social reciprocity. It allows individuals to understand the thoughts and feelings of persons from cultures other than their own. It is no gainsaying that social reality is experienced differently from different ethnic and social class positions. Thus, we must begin to look at film as "texts" that rely on visual imagery to tell specific stories, and is in the business of promoting specific ideologies. Textual interpretation of film, therefore, requires skills that can allow you to discover the deeper meanings embedded in the film as a text. One basic fact we have to understand is that not all films are meant to "entertain," (such as avant-garde films). Like any other works of art, it is meant to inform, educate, entertain and mobilize.

We also have to recognize that films are made to be seen and heard, to appeal to our visual and aural senses. Like any art form, however, films are also meant to be felt and understood, to appeal to our emotions and minds. One of the best ways to determine whether a film has succeeded in any or all of these goals is to analyze the elements that make up the whole work.

The film critic, Christian Metz, once observed that "A film is difficult to explain because it is easy to understand." Fact is, we are used to sitting back in the dark and viewing a film uncritically; indeed, most Hollywood films are constructed to render "invisible" the carefully constructed nature of the medium. Further, because a film is constructed of visual, aural, and linguistic components that are manipulated in numerous ways, it is a challenge to take apart the totality of the film experience and to interpret how that experience was assembled. To write an analysis of a film, you must study the film carefully. Your critical analysis should be derived from your personal encounter with the film, not from published criticisms. In writing an analysis of a film, it is not enough to like or dislike the movie; you must determine why it succeeds or fails in reaching out and encompassing the viewer.

Before Undertaking Analysis of a Film

1. Before writing an analysis and interpretation of a film, it is important to view the film in its entirety. From this viewing you can get an initial reaction to the many parts of the film that you will have to explore in more depth. When you first view the film, it is best not to try to take notes or separate the parts of the film; you should be familiar with the film in order to know what to look for. Thereafter, you have to formulate a thesis and locate evidences that support the thesis.

2. Note that the thesis statement is the element around which to structure your analysis. Since the theme or focus of the film is basically the thesis of the filmmaker, identification of that theme can often serve as the thesis of the film analysis itself.

3. After identifying the thesis or theme, you have to look at the remainder of the elements of the film in light of their success or failure to support the film's central focus.

4. After determining the thesis, you should view the film again with an eye on noting particular elements used by the filmmaker. At this point you can take a more critical and in-depth look at story, dramatic structure, symbolism, characterization, conflict, and other fictional or dramatic elements. It is important to describe in detail scenes or portions of the film where these elements are used and to discuss their contribution to the film's overall success or failure.

The above-mentioned steps are critical to any literary analysis. The visual and aural elements of a film are the basic means of communication in a film. The artistic use of the visual and aural qualities and properties of the film medium determines the effectiveness of the film. Although it is impossible to look at every visual and aural element employed in a film, the use of a VCR or laserdisc or DVD player will enable you to pinpoint and examine the filmmaker's use of camera angles and camera movement, focus, framing, lighting, setting, editing, point of view, special effects, dialogue, and music. After exploring these major cinematic elements and describing specific examples of their use, it is necessary to relate all of these examples and elements to the thesis of your analysis. At this point, the use of smooth and clear transitions is vital to the paper's success.

An analysis of a film should be basically objective, and such a critical analysis should include your personal reactions to the film and explain your reasons for liking or disliking it. Even if the film does not meet your expectations, your analysis should explain how successful the film was in reaching its own level of ambition and in achieving its aims. After completing the film analysis, you probably will not change your immediate reaction to the film. But you are likely to have a better understanding and appreciation of that reaction and the effects of the film on viewers in general. It is import for students of Film to know the difference between Reviews, Criticism and Analysis and Interpretation.

Difference between Film Review, Interpretation and Criticism

While the terms "review" and "criticism" are often used interchangeably, there are differences between them. Note how motion pictures are often referred to as "films" when discussing criticism, and "movies" when discussing reviews.

Film criticism is the study, interpretation, and evaluation of a film and its place in cinema history. Film criticism usually offers interpretation of its meaning, analysis of its structure and style, judgment of its worth by comparison with other films, and an estimation of its likely effect on viewers. Film theory (e.g., feminist, postmodernist, etc.) often informs the critical analysis of a film. Criticism may examine a particular film, or may look at a group of films in the same genre, or a director's or actor's body of work.

Film criticism differs from movie reviews in several ways: it entails both analysis and judgment; it may be published many years after a film is released; it is usually longer and more complex than a movie review. Serious film criticism, whether essays written for magazines, journals, books, or class assignments, attempts to analyze films, rather than merely review them or provide simple descriptions of what happens.

A *review* (perhaps 400-1200 words) typically includes **personal impressions** and **evaluations** of a movie's content and techniques. A good review may touch superficially on topics that might be explored in more detail in a longer formal analysis. A review documents the critical reception of a film at its time of theatrical or DVD release. It is more "consumer-oriented," placing more emphasis on recommendation than analysis. Reviews of feature films or mainstream films may be found in online databases, newspapers, and general interest magazines (e.g., *New York Times*, *Daily Graphic, Ghanaian Times, Village Voice*, *Cineaste, The Sun etc.*).

In-depth criticism and analyses of some feature films or mainstream films, foreign films, independent films, documentaries, etc. may be found in more scholarly or academic publications (e.g., *Film Quarterly*, *Cinema Journal*, *and Film International*).

Film Analysis and Interpretation

An *analysis* (perhaps 1200-12,000 words) attempts to determine how the film actually uses various cinematic techniques and elements of film or narrative form to make a viewer react in a certain way and why it makes viewers come away with certain opinions about it. When we interpret a text or film, are we uncovering a hidden meaning? Or are we imposing on the text or film a meaning from the outside? But the question is: how are interpretations made? In interpreting a film, the critic essentially reconstructs it, creating a "model film" – a mental version which downplays or ignores certain elements while highlighting others, all "unified under a description which organizes those aspects of the film he or she has picked out and weighted with semantic values. The difference between a critic and an ordinary spectator is that while the average moviegoer may have a jumble of free floating thoughts and associations, a critic must work to create a thorough interpretation that is convincing according to the tacit standards of the interpretative institution of which they are a part. An analysis requires some reflective thought about the film, and usually benefits from multiple viewings and outside research.

Writing a Literary Criticism

In general, a literary critique is a genre of academic writing that briefly summarizes and critically evaluates a work or concept in a work. Critiques can be used to carefully analyze a variety of works such as:

1. **Creative works** – novels, exhibits, film, images, poetry

2. **Research** – monographs, journal articles, systematic reviews, theories

3. **Media** – news reports, feature articles

Like an essay, a critique uses a formal, academic writing style and has a clear structure, that is, an introduction, body and conclusion. However, the body of a critique includes a summary of the work and a detailed evaluation. The purpose of an evaluation is to gauge the usefulness or impact of a work in a particular field.

Why do we write critiques?

Writing a critique on a work helps us to develop:

1. Knowledge of the work's subject area or related works.

2. An understanding of the work's purpose, intended audience, development of argument, structure of evidence or creative style.

3. Recognition of the strengths and weaknesses of the work.

Notes on How to write a critique

Before you start writing, it is important to have a thorough understanding of the work that will be critiqued.

1. Study the work under discussion.

2. Make notes on key parts of the work.

3. Develop an understanding of the main argument or purpose being expressed in the work.

4. Consider how the work relates to a broader issue or context.

Format for Analyzing, Critiquing and Interpreting Film

There are a variety of ways to structure the analysis or critique of a film. You should always check with your lecturer for guidance depending on your discipline. Sometimes, your lecturer will indicate the length of the essay. The following template, which showcases the main features of a critique, is provided as one example.

A. Introduction

Normally, the introduction is short (less than 10-15% of the length of the essay) and should embody the following:

1. Name the work being analyzed or reviewed as well as the date it was created and the name of the author/creator.

2. Describe the main argument or purpose of the film.

3. Explain the context in which the film was created. This could include the social or political context, the place of the work in a creative or academic tradition, or the relationship between the work and the creator's life experience.

4. Have a concluding sentence that signposts what your evaluation of the work will be. For instance, it may indicate whether it is a positive, negative, or mixed evaluation.

B. Summary

Briefly summarize the main points and objectively describe how the creator portrays these by using techniques, styles, media, characters or symbols. This summary should not be the focus of the critique and is usually shorter than the critical evaluation. **In other words, provide the artistic use of the visual and aural qualities and properties of the film.**

C. Critical evaluation

This section should give a systematic and detailed assessment of the different elements of the work, evaluating how well the creator was able to achieve the purpose through these. For example: as you would assess the plot structure, characterization and setting of a novel; an assessment of a painting would look at composition, brush strokes, color and light; a critique of a research project would look at subject selection, design of the experiment, analysis of data and conclusions.

A critical evaluation does not simply highlight negative impressions. It should **deconstruct** the work and **identify both strengths and weaknesses**. It should examine the work and evaluate its success, in light of its purpose.

Examples of key critical questions that could help your assessment include:

1. Who is the creator? Is the work presented objectively or subjectively?

2. What are the aims of the work? Were the aims achieved?

3. What techniques, styles, media were used in the work? Are they effective in portraying the purpose?

4. What assumptions underlie the work? Do they affect its validity?

5. What types of evidence or persuasion are used? Has evidence been interpreted fairly?

6. How is the work structured? Does it favor a particular interpretation or point of view? Is it effective?

7. Does the work enhance understanding of key ideas or theories? Does the work engage (or fail to engage) with key concepts or other works in its discipline?

NOTE WELL: The evaluation should be written in formal academic style and language, and logically presented. Group and order your ideas into paragraphs. Start with the broad impressions first and then move into the details of the technical elements. For shorter critiques, you may discuss the strengths of the works, and then the weaknesses. In longer critiques, you may wish to discuss the positive and negative of each key critical question in individual paragraphs.

To support the evaluation, **provide evidence from the work itself**, such as a quote or example, and you should also cite evidence from related sources. Explain how this evidence supports your evaluation of the work.

D. Conclusion

This is usually a very brief paragraph, which includes:

1. A statement indicating the overall evaluation of the work

2. A summary of the key reasons, identified during the critical evaluation, why this evaluation was formed.

3. In some circumstances, recommendations for improvement on the work may be appropriate.

E. Works Cited/References

Include all resources cited in your critique. Check with your lecturer for which referencing style to use.

(Adapted from QUT, http://www.citewrite.qut.edu.au/write/critique.jsp)

Things a Film Critic Should Know

1. When one watches a film, movie or video, one might argue that the more entertaining a film is the more effective it is at conveying its underlying meaning, for viewers are more resistant to having their enjoyment impinged upon by raising ideological concerns. However, given that a film is meant to reach a broad mainstream audience, its messages could be subversive or meant to maintain mainstream ideas about gender, sexism, ideology, class, consumerism, the media etc.

2. A film or movie may be an adaptation of a novel or a given text. Sometimes, the director of the film may alter the theme and it may reflect something different from the theme of the novel or text being adapted. Therefore, you need to delve deeper than the literal or surface meaning in your understanding of the film.

3. Films are meant to educate, inform entertain and motivate. They are documents of their time and place, as well as artistic forms of self-expression. Films or movies we see at theatres, on television, or on home video are typically *narrative* films. They tell stories about characters going through life experiences. But what are they really about? What is the *content* of a film?

Expectations and What it means to analyze a Film

When you are asked to write or analyze a film at college level, you are being asked to do the following:

1. Describe or summarize the film or something
2. Analyze and interpret it
3. Evaluate it
4. Relate it to scholarship, to themes or subject in human experience.

The overall idea, when analyzing a film is to look for anything that is repeated (the first 10 minutes are the most important):

1. Images or symbols
2. Colors
3. Words or phrases
4. Entire lines of dialogue
5. Camera angles or camera movement
6. Lighting
7. Props or items of clothing
8. An actor's posture, gestures, or movement

No matter how bad the movie is, there are repeated items that can be found, and once these repeated items are discovered, the key is to ask: "what are their overall meaning?" Finally, "What is this film *really* about?" Below are four basic formats for analyzing a film.

Format 1

A. Paragraph One: Introduction

B. Paragraph Two. Summary of Main Points

C. Paragraph Three. Summary of Content

D. Paragraph Four. Summary of Content / Evaluation

E. Paragraph Five. Analysis of Text

F. Paragraph Six. Evaluation of Text

G Paragraph Seven. Analysis/Evaluation

H. Paragraph Eight. Evaluation of Text as a Whole

I. Works Cited/References

Format 2

1. Introduction: Title of the film, who wrote or directed the film? What is the setting of the film? What is the subject matter of the film? A little summary.

2. Body: What is the structure of the film? What comes first, second, third? How does the author build her/his argument or plot?

3. Body: How does the director or the author deal with the characters? What evidence is used to support claims of the characters? Which characters dominate? Does characterization in any way "predetermine" certain conclusions? In the film, what kind of language, descriptions, or sections of plot alert you to the themes and significance of the film?

4. Body: What are the subject matter, argument, and possible theme of the film? What major claims or conclusions does the director or writer make? What issues does the film illuminate? What attitude to life does it present?

5. **Body:** What is the writer or director's purpose, position?

6. **Body:** What did the director or author ignore or leave out?

7. **Body:** What are my responses, attitudes and experiences?

8. **Body:** What relevant scholarship is out there about the issues being discussed in the film?

9. **Conclusion:** Does the film contribute to world view, scholarship?

10. **Works Cited/References:** Include all resources cited in your critique. Check with your lecturer/tutor for which referencing style to use.

Format 3

I. Introduction

Do exactly what you would do if you were standing in front of an audience: introduce what you will review, the author, and the points you intend to make about this work.

a. Give relevant bibliographic information;

b. Give the reader a clear idea of the nature, scope, and significance of the work;

c. Indicate your evaluation of the work in a clear 1-2 sentence thesis statement.

Provide background information to help your readers understand the importance of the work or the reasons for your appraisal. Some examples follow:

a. Explain why the issue examined is of current interest;

b. Tell what scholarship says about this subject;

c. Describe the author's perspective, methodology, purpose;

d. Give information concerning the circumstances under which the book or film was created.

II. Summary

Summarize the contents very briefly:

a. Focus on the main points and purposes of the work;

b. Focus also on the ideas, themes, or arguments that you will evaluate or discuss later.

Tip: Keep it short! A paragraph or two should be sufficient.

III. Analysis/Evaluation

Analyze and explain the significance of the main points of the work. Evaluate the work, answering questions such as the following:

a. Does the work do what its author claimed it would?

b. Leaving out your points of agreement or disagreement, is the work valid and accurate?

c. What are your reasons for agreeing, disagreeing, liking, disliking, believing, disbelieving?

IV. Conclusion/Recommendation

Give your overall assessment of the work. Drive home your chief point.

V. Works Cited/References: Include all resources cited in your critique. Check with your lecturer/tutor for which referencing style to use.

Format 4

Paragraph 1: Offer your overall impression of the film while mentioning the movie's title,

director, and key actors.

Paragraph 2: Summarize the plot of the film

Paragraph 3: How did the actors portray key character roles? Did they fulfill your expectations

given your knowledge of the original novel or play (if one exists)?

Paragraph 4: Were any particular film techniques used in key scenes? How did the film

techniques and music enhance the setting and themes of the film? You may need two paragraphs to explain this information.

Paragraph 5: Address how well the film represents the novel or play. Offer evidence for your

opinion. Remember to mention use of symbols and literary devices. Do they "transfer" from the novel/play into the movie well?

Paragraph 6: Ending paragraph—your last opportunity to guide the reader. Offer a clincher that

tells the reader to attend the film or not.

Works Cited/References: Include all resources cited in your critique. Check with your lecturer/tutor for which referencing style to use.

(Adapted from "Guidelines" by M. Garbis and C. Adams, Baltimore, 2001.)

In conclusion, a film, is not a static medium, thus its stories are much more complex. Analyzing a film, then, is much **more than** "reading a novel." In short, analyzing a film requires you to take a careful look at the setting, plot, characters, dialogue, symbols, metaphors, archetypes, etc., as well as those factors that have an influence on the film, such as the social, historical, and political context in which the film was created.

Revision: Before You Analyze or Interpret a Film

In sum, in order to do textual analysis of a film, one needs to acquire the technical and formalist language of film studies. These are the tools to use to explore the text for meanings beyond the basic level of plot, dialogue and character development, which are how most audiences, not trained in film analysis, "understand" the film. You also need to go beyond what our immediate response to a film might be. A good interpretation can be made only by referring to direct evidence to support arguments about the film (as in a text), using the analytical tools of film studies. It's not enough simply to have a gut-level reaction that something doesn't "make sense"—you need to refer to the text. When considering the characters in a film, remember that they are not real people with real motivations beyond what is in the text.

Motivations cannot be analyzed simply by referring to one's own experience, although they may be a starting point. Rather, you have to consider why a character appears to be motivated to do what he or she does in the film (or in some cases, why there is no apparent motivation at all) within the structure of the film. This is a basic part of narrative analysis. But discovering the basic narrative structures around motivation are simply the first step—plot summary. You need to keep asking yourself, what the motivations of the characters mean in terms of the larger interpretation of the film. In addition, how does the film "works" to create its effects on audiences, and what the film "means."

The Dos and Don'ts about analyzing of a film

At college, you will most likely be asked to write essays, reviews or analysis of films, books, or articles and to model these reviews or so on ones published in scholarly journals. Even among these reviews, however, there is a great deal of variety. There is the short book review, sometimes called a **capsule review**, which is usually less than five hundred words long and which focuses mainly on giving readers who have not read the reviewed book in order to have a grip of the general sense of its content and value. The goal is to encourage each student to relate the ideas of others to the themes of a subject, discipline, and to his or her own thinking about a film assigned to the class.

Critical ideas to keep in mind while writing this essay include (a) In what way does this film contribute to scholarship? (b) How does that film broaden the understanding of issues in society i.e. socialization, global warming etc.? (c) What does the film connects with in human life or society?

A review is not a research paper

Some students, instead of writing about a book or a film when they are asked to analyze or to write a review, write a research paper on the subject of the book or film.

A review is not a summary

It is important to summarize the contents and significance of whatever you analyze or review. But at university, the review is more than a description or summary. The review is an evaluation, a critical analysis, a commentary.

A review is not a book

Don't make the mistake of re-telling the film in your own words. You don't have the time or space, and this approach doesn't allow you to express your interpretation or evaluation. Remember, in an academic setting, your audience could very well have seen the film, so what is wanted is not a detailed description but the communication of your own critical analysis and judgment.

A review is not a book report

A book report does give a fairly detailed description of the contents of a book. It may also provide background information about the book: who wrote it, when it was published, or how popular it was, for example. A review analyzes, interprets, and evaluates.

A review is not an off-the-cuff, unfair personal response

Writing an essay or analyzing a film involves communicating your personal view about the film. General, flip statements that don't express your understanding of what you have seen are next to useless. Comments like "I thought the book was interesting." "The movie was boring" are not sufficient. Why was the film interesting, boring, or challenging? Did it reveal some new insights/information? Was the director trying to produce a boring movie to realistically depict life in the revolution?

A review is not a string of quotations

Although quotations from a text or from the dialogue of a film may be useful, they do not explain your thinking or judgments. So use quotations sparingly. By the way, using quotations from other reviews are not a good idea: you are supposed to be writing the analysis essay, not compiling other's opinions.

Works Cited/References: Remember to include all resources cited in your analysis or critique. Check with your lecturer for which referencing style to use.

Other Things to know about Analyzing Film

According to Goldberg, when analyzing a film as a historical document, keep in mind the film's contemporary audiences or authors. Your own personal reaction to the film may serve as a starting point, but you need to convert these impressions into historical analysis—how are you different and similar to the historical audiences/authors? What has changed and what has stayed the same? Remember too, the technological changes that have taken place, and keep in mind what audiences would have expected, and how film makers used the technology at their disposal. It is especially important to consider substantial changes in the manner of presentation if you will only be watching the film on a television. Also, be aware that most Hollywood films made after the early 1950s have an "aspect ratio" (height and width ratio) different from television screens. Most video tapes of these films have been altered by the "pan and scan" method which dramatically changes elements such as shot composition and camera movement. Video tapes that are "widescreen" preserve the correct aspect ratio. Most DVDs now come in both "standard" (altered) and "widescreen" (check the writing on the disk) or only in the correct aspect ratio and most laser disks use the correct aspect ratio. If possible, find a format that has not altered the aspect ratio. When writing an academic essay, which is an analysis essay about a film, Goldberg suggests the following elaborations to assist in the approach to the analysis essay:

A. MEANING

1. **Themes/tropes—**The broad ideas and allusions (themes) that are established by repetition of technical and linguistic means (tropes) throughout the film (such as alienation, power and control, transcendence through romantic achievement, etc.)

2. **Intent/Message—**Sometimes, as with a film like *JFK* (the Kennedy assassination was the result of a massive government conspiracy) or *Wayne's World* (adolescence is a goofy time that provides plenty of laughs), this is obvious. (Just because the message is obvious, doesn't mean that the film is simple or that there is not a contradictory subtext). Sometimes, however, the filmmakers aren't sure of their message, or the intended message becomes clouded along the way. At other times, the filmmakers (principally the producer, director, actors and actresses) are at odds over the intent. At other times, the film makers intend one message and many in the audience interpret the film differently.)

3. **Metaphor and metonymy/symbolism—**Similar to literary interpretation, only consider all aspects of the film—linguistic, visual,

aural. Metaphors are elements that represent something different from their explicit meaning (for example, the rose petals in American Beauty). Metonyms are elements that are similar or the same (for example, in the final scene of The Grapes of Wrath, Tom Joad represents the lonely battle of activists and Ma represents the resilience of "the people"; or when a part of the whole—such as a close-up of a woman's leg—represents women as sexual objects). Metaphors and metonyms only gain relevance if they are repeated in significant ways or connected with the larger meaning of the film. (Avoid simplistic equations such as the white table symbolizes A; the high angle shot of a character symbolized B).

4. Subtext—The often numerous messages a film conveys beneath the surface; sometimes intended, often unintended, and sometimes conveying a different or contradictory message than the intended message. Look especially for ironies, contradictions, interesting juxtapositions, or if something initially doesn't seem to "make sense." Subtext is usually developed through the use of figurative elements like metaphor and metonymy.

B. BASIC ELEMENTS

1. Title/opening credits—Titles are chosen carefully—consider alternatives and why this title was chosen; consider ambiguities in the title ("His Girl Friday," a film with a strong, independent female protagonist). The opening credits establish a tone, and often are used to foreshadow events, themes, or metaphors—pay careful attention from the beginning.

2. Story/Plot/Narrative—The narrative provides the basic structure by which a feature film is understood. (Most documentaries also have narratives.) The narrative consists of the story and the plot. The story consists of all of the information conveyed by the film (either directly or by inference) assembled in chronological order to communicate the overall sense of what occurred in the film. The ***diegesis*** is the entire world of the story. A film's diegesis may have a different logic than the "real" world, but as long as there is proper motivation, it will make sense to the viewer. Diegetic elements are found explicitly or implicitly in the world of the story; non- or extra-diegetic elements (the soundtrack, the title, a voice-over, an audience's expectations of a star's persona) are outside the story. The plot provides the cause and effect relations that cue the audience and create suspense, surprise, and fulfill expectations. While dialogue provides a good deal of information, pay attention to all the other audio and visual clues that convey information about the narrative. In considering the narrative structure, note whether the film follows a standard chronological narrative or not and how time is used. What are the key moments and how are they established? What are the climaxes and anticlimaxes? How far ahead the audience in understanding what is happening to the characters than the characters themselves are? What propels the story forward? What is the pace of the narrative? How do earlier parts of the narrative set up later parts? Where are the key emotive moments, when the audience is frightened, enraged, enraptured, feeling vindicated, etc., and how has the narrative helped to establish these feelings? Note, when there is a *change of knowledge* (when characters or the audience become aware of new information) it shifts the *hierarchy of knowledge* (the relative amount of knowledge characters and the audience have). Does the narrative have a coherent unity, or does it leave the audience feeling unfulfilled or confused? (Sometimes the latter is the mark of an unsuccessful film; sometimes it's either an intentional effect to challenge the easy "Hollywood ending" or else the result of the mixed intentions of the various authors).

3. **Motivation—**"Justification given in the film for the presence of an element. This may appeal to the viewer's knowledge of the real world, to genre conventions, to narrative causality, or to a stylistic pattern within the film" (Bordwell, Thompson). Failure to provide proper motivation challenges the sense of "cinematic realism" in a film. (If a character's personal motivation is explained in a film as a reason for

his/her action that falls under "narrative causality." Do not confuse character motivation as revealed through narrative with your own expectations you bring to the film. Characters are not real people, and do not make choices outside of what is conveyed narratively.) Hollywood films tend to stress perfectly motivated narratives so that every element has a purpose. Discovering the underlying motivation of the narrative often helps explain why audience expectations are fulfilled (or if poorly motivated, unfulfilled.) For example, in the Western *Unforgiven*, the close-up, eerily lighted shot of Morgan Freeman's/Ned's scars from whipping by Gene Hackman/Little Bill motivates Clint Eastwood's/ William Money's slaughter of Hackman and various townsfolk. The shot thus cues the audience's desire for revenge through violence (note the metonymic symbolism of the scarred black body and the whip), despite the supposedly anti-violent theme of the film.

4. Motif—The repetition of an element in ways that acquire symbolic meaning for the element. A motif can be a technical feature (a shot angle, a lighting set up), a sound or piece of dialogue or music, or an object.

5. Parallelism—Two or more scenes that are similar to each other but which gain meaning because of their differences.

6. Characterization—Who are the central characters? How are minor characters used? Are characters thinly or fully drawn, and why? Who in the audience is meant to relate to which characters, and what sort of emotion (fear, pleasure, anxiety) are audience members meant to feel because of this identification? Is there a clear or ambivalent hero or villain? What values do the characters represent, and do they change during the film? Are the characters meant to play a particular "type" and do they play against type at any time?

7. Point of view—Is the film in general told from a particular character's point of view, or is it "objective"? Is the film's perspective primarily intellectual or emotional, visionary or "realistic"? Within the

film, is a particular shot viewed from a character's point of view ("subjective shot"), and how does the camera technically reinforce the point of view? Who is the audience meant to be focusing on at a particular moment?

C. MISE-EN-SCENE—it is everything going on within the frame outside of editing and sounds.

1. Setting and sets—is the scene shot in a studio sound stage or "on location"? How is the setting integrated into the action, both the larger background and particular props? How is the setting used in composing the shot (verticals and horizontals, windows and doors, the ever popular slats of shades, mirrors, etc.)? How do particular settings (vast mountain ranges, cluttered urban setting) function as signs in order to convey narrative and ideological information? How are colors used?

2. Acting style—more obviously mannered ("classical"); intense and psychologically driven ("method"); less affectations and more "natural"? Do particular actors have their own recognizable style or type, and how do the filmmakers use the audience's expectations, either by reaffirming or challenging these expectations? What expectations do "stars" bring to their roles? Do they fulfill or challenge these expectations (playing against type)?

3. Costumes (or lack thereof)—note contrasts between characters, changes within film; use of colors. This also includes physiques, hair styles, etc.

4. Lighting—*Key Light*: the main lighting, usually placed at a 45-degree angle between camera and subject. *Fill Light*: Auxiliary lights, usually from the side of the subject that softens or eliminates shadows and illuminates areas not covered by the Key Light. High Key Lighting is when all the lights are on (typical of musicals and comedies); *Low Key* Lighting is when one or more of the fill lighting is eliminated, creating more opportunity for shadows. High contrast lighting refers to sharp contrast between light and dark; low contrast refers to shades of gray.

Hard lighting creates a harsh light; soft lighting creates a muted, usually more forgiving lighting. "Hard" characters often get hard lighting, and vice versa. Highlighting or spotlighting: pencil-thin beams of light used to illuminate certain parts of a subject, often eyes or other facial features. Backlighting: placing the main source of light behind the subject, silhouetting it, and directing the light toward the camera. *Top-lighting*: lighting from above. Lighting and camera angle are the key means of creating shadows and shadings in black and white films, which are important elements of the overall "mise-en-scene" when conveying meaning. All of the above terms are bipolar, when in fact many lighting setups lie somewhere in between.

5. Diffuser/Filter: A gelatin plate that is placed in front of light to change the effect. (Whether to cast a shadow or soften the light, for instance.)

E. Cinematography—The camera work that records the mise-en-scene between edits. Each shot represents many choices made by the film makers. Why have they made these choices? What do these choices represent?

1. Tone—bright, sharp colors; grainy and black and white: hazy? If black and white when color was available, why would the film makers make this choice?

2. Film speed—slow or fast motion used? film speed reversed?

3. Camera Angle—The angle at which the camera is pointed at the subject: low (shot from below), high (shot from above), or eye-level (includes extreme low and high angle shots). This creates the angle of vision—the point of view—for the audience, and is often used to establish character's level of power and control (high angle shots can make character seem diminished), but there are many other uses as well.

4. Tracking, Panning, and Tilt—Tracking shot moves the camera either sideways or in and out. The camera can be mounted on a "dolly,"

"handheld" to create a jerkier effect, mounted on a crane and moved in all directions within a limited range, or in a helicopter, train, car, plane, etc. for other effects. Panning swings the camera horizontally, tilt swigs it vertically. These effects are often used simultaneously.

5. Angle of View/lens—The angle of the shot created by the lens. A wide angle lens presents broad views of subjects, and makes possible a large depth of field (many planes of action) as well as a deep focus shot. A normal lens (35 mm) can only focus on one plane at a time. A telephoto lens has a very narrow angle of views which acts like a telescope to focus faraway subjects and flattens the view.

6. Focus—"Shallow focus" uses sharp focus on the characters or things in one area of the shot and soft (blurred) focus in the rest. "Deep focus" brings out the detail in all areas of the shot. "Focus In" gradually "zooms" in on the subject, "focus out" gradually "zooms" out (these are known as "focus pulls"). Rack focus is an extremely fast focus pull that changes focus from one image/character to another by changing the focus to a different plane.

7. Shot distance—Full shot, three-quarters shot, mid- or half-shot, close-up and extreme close-up for shots of bodies; (extreme) long-shot, mid-shot, (extreme) close-up to describe more general. Can be used to create sense of isolation (extreme long shot of character in a desert) or great pain, anger or joy (extreme close-up of character's face). Choice of lens (see above) can create strange effects (wide angle close up extends and distorts image at the edges, like a funhouse mirror; telephoto lens used in long shots flatten distances and putting background out of focus.

8. Frame—the border that contains the image. Can be "open" (with characters moving in and out); "moving" (using focus, tracking, panning); "canted" (at odd angles, unbalanced shot composition).

9. Shot composition—The relation of the elements of mise-en-scene to the frame. Small frames used with close-ups can create sense

of claustrophobia, often enhanced by the set (low ceilings, numerous props and furnishings) and lighting. The set can also be used to frame the shot in other ways (lamps, flags, etc. on either side; a bed out-of-focus at the bottom of the frame) as can characters (as signs of intimidation, marginality, support, etc.) These types of shots are unbalanced. Look also for shots that are perfectly symmetrical.

F. Montage—Editing ("cuts") within scenes and in the film in general, creating continuities and discontinuities, juxtapositions, and narrative structure. The standard Hollywood practice is to make cuts "invisible," and thus they are often difficult to pick up within a scene. "Montage" is also the term used for a series of quick cuts from a variety of locations that cohere narratively or thematically (the baptism scene in *The Godfather I* is a good example). "Accelerated montage" is what it sounds like (the prison escape scene in *His Girl Friday*).

1. Editing pace—within a sequence, from long takes (the opening credits of The Graduate) to "accelerated montage" (the chase scene of Bullit); within the film in general, to establish overall tone. Since the "natural" state of a Hollywood film movement, long takes coupled with a still camera can be used to increase intensity of a shot, make the audience uncomfortable, etc.

2. Establishing shot—Initial shot in a scene that establishes location, characters, and purpose of the scene.

3. Shot/counter shot—standard device used during dialogue between two characters; often starts with a "two-shot" of the two characters, then moves back and forth. Combined with camera angle, shot distance, and pace to establish point of view. Note when this standard device is not used, and for what purpose. Note when the person speaking is not viewed, or only back is viewed.

4. Reaction shot—Quick cut to pick up character's reaction to an event. Lack of reaction shot when it seems logical should be noted.

5. Jump Cut—A cut that occurs within a scene (rather than

between scenes) that removes part of a shot. This shot is often done for effect by making the cut obvious and disrupting the invisible editing of Hollywood style.

6. Freeze Frame—A freeze shot, which is achieved by printing a single frame many times in succession to give the illusion of a still photograph.

7. Crosscutting—A shot inserted in a scene to show action happening elsewhere at the same time.

8. Cutaway—A cut within a shot to a location that links the action of the shot and condenses time (for example, a reaction shot of a woman watching a man climb some stairs, cutting out a flight in between the shots).

9. Match Cut—A cut in which two shots are linked by visual, aural, or metaphorical parallelism.

10. Scenes—An end of a scene is usually marked by a number of possible devices, including fade-ins and fade-outs (which may include a quick cut or a fade to black—note the length of time the blackout is maintained, which often implies significance of preceding scene, or else a long passage of time); wipe (a line moves across the screen, usually used in older films); dissolve (a new shot briefly superimposed on an old shot), often used to express continuity or connections

11. Sequence—A series of scenes that fit together narratively or representationally

12. Accelerated montage—a series of quick cuts that relate a variety of shots from different locations into a coherent story or not

G. Sound—Sometimes non-dialogue sound is the hardest element to pick out and analyze, yet is often extremely important and subject to just as much of the film makers focus as other elements. Note how sound is used—to underscore emotions, to alert the audience to an upcoming event, as an ironic counterpoint, etc. Carefully created and edited sounds (including the use of silences) create a rich aural images the same way that mise-en-scene, shot composition, and montage creates visual images. Note that sound is both part of the mise-en-scene and is a separate category of editing (since the audio track is separate from the video track).

1. Dialogue—Is it overlapping, mumbled, very soft or loud?

2. Sound effects—both the effects themselves (a doorbell ringing) and the manipulation of the sound (stereo effects which move sounds across the sound spectrum, or balance sounds on one side or the other; filtering and manipulating sounds).

3. Score—the background music used throughout the film. The score often maintains and manipulates a similar theme at various times (especially in older films), and is often used in relation to the narrative structure. Particular *motifs* or themes may be used in relation to particular characters.

4. Sound Bridge—Connects scenes or sequences by a sound that continues through the visual transition.

5. Direct sound refers to sound that is recorded at the time the scene is shot (usually dialogue, although audio inserts are possible. All audio inserts would be post-synchronous sound.).

6. Post-synchronous sound refers to sound that is recorded and placed on the film audio track after the scene is shot (virtually all scores). Most non-dialogue sounds are inserted after production (for example, footsteps), as well as a fair amount of dialogue that is either inserted when characters are not shown speaking onscreen, or simply pasted over sections that they are deemed to need improvement.

7. Diegetic sound is heard within the film's diegesis (dialogue, a shot from a gun on screen).

8. Off-screen sound appears within the film's diegesis but not within the frame (extending off-screen space).

9. Non-diegetic sound is heard outside of the film's diegesis (such as film scores and voice-overs). A pop song that seems to be part of the soundtrack but is found to be coming from, say, a car radio, is a diegetic sound and is an element worth noting.

10. Simultaneous sound is heard at the same time the action happens on screen.

11. Non-simultaneous sound is heard before or after the action happens on-screen.

G. Works Cited

Include all resources cited in your critique. Check with your lecturer for which referencing style to use.

(Adapted from a format designed by Michael Goldberg: https://faculty.washington.edu/mlg/students/readafilm.htm 9/14/00)

Chapter Ten

Writing an Analysis about a Dance Performance

What to look for in a Dance Performance?

a) When writing a dance critique, there are many things to consider prior to the performance. Who is performing? Are they professionals or amateurs? Is it a new work or classic choreography reset? Who are the choreographers? Are they known for other works? It is important to meditate carefully on the performance prior to seeing it so you can take as much from it as you can.

b) When viewing a performance be an active participant, don't be a passive consumer. Work as hard at viewing the piece as the choreographer did making the work. Consult your program notes when writing critiques.

c) During the performance, there are also many things to consider that should be incorporated into your writing process. What style of dance is it? Is the performance experimental or conventional? What are the cultural implications of the performance? How do elements of the performance, such as lighting, scenery, and costume, enhance the choreography?

d) If a performance is very abstract, take as much from it as you can and strive to deliver your opinion of it as clearly as possible in your writing. Remember that there is no right answer since art is abstract and everyone responds to art differently.

e) There is a lot to take in when viewing dance, and it can be easy to forget aspects of the performance. It is helpful to bring a notebook and pen to jot down notes and initial reactions to the performance that you may forget later on. Also, write the paper as soon as possible after the performance to prevent a foggy recollection.

f) If there is a talk-back at the end of the performance, at which the choreographers and/or dancers answer questions and explain the performance more thoroughly, it is highly advisable to stay. It can offer you some insight into the choreographer's motivation as well as uncover some of the meaning of the performance.

Guidelines for Writing About a Dance Performance

a) The opening statement of your critique should draw the reader in. Be creative. Tell the reader where and when the concert took place.

b) When writing about choreographers, always identify them by name. Try to get inside the head of the choreographer. What were the choreographer's intentions and were they successfully communicated? What do you think the choreographer was trying to say with the dance, or what did the dance say? Try to have a thematic focus when writing your critique. Were the themes of the individual piece clear? What was the dance about? Analyze the symbolism. Does it relate to current events?

c) Discuss the choreography. Did the choreography flow, what were the dynamics, how did it move in space and what were the motivations for the movements? Make general comments but also include detailed descriptions. Try to give at least one specific movement image. Example: "In another vignette, a woman seated properly, perpendicularly, on a bench, begins to tilt at an angle. As her legs leave the floor and her torso leans to the side, both she and the bench seem to levitate a little above the floor." Vienna-Lusthaus (revisited); Reviewed by George Jackson: Dance Magazine, May 2003: 79.

d) What thoughts or feelings did the concert or piece evoke? In constructing your critique, reflect on why you may have had certain reactions. Always back up your assertions, positive or negative with concrete examples. Don't just be a negative critic; offer your thoughts in a constructive way.

e) Comment on the music and identify the composer(s) and musician(s) when possible. What was the relationship of the dance to the music? Did the music play an important role in the performance? Was the music live, pre-recorded or some combination of both? What difference did it make? Did the form of the music influence the form of the dance or vice versa?

f) Were the dances well-rehearsed and/or well performed? Support your comments with specific examples. Did the dancers work together well in the ensemble pieces?

g) Were the makeup, props (if used), and costumes appropriate? Discuss the scenic design, lighting design, and overall use of the theatre space. **When speaking about any element of design, you must include the designers' names.**

h) Comment on the overall production; give the reader a sense of what it looked like. What was your reaction to the concert as a whole? How did the piece or pieces connect?

i) Each critique should reach a conclusion regarding the performance.

Mechanics:

a) Do not write in the first person. Your critique should be written in the third person.

b) Your essay, paying attention to grammar, neatness and spelling, should be as thorough as possible.

c) All critiques must have a title page, which will include name, date, professor's name, course and the pledge written in full and signed.

d) The ticket stub and/or verification from the performance must be attached to each critique.

e) Only typed papers, three pages, double-spaced, in standard 12 font, with one inch margins on all sides, are acceptable; do not justify right margin. Check your computer for margin settings.

f) Student's last name and page number should be included in the upper right corner of each page.

g) Critiques are due the second class following the performance. Read other critiques in *Dance Magazine*, if necessary.

h) Tell the reader the name of the performance, the company or dancers performing, the date and place of the performance.

i) Identify the composer(s), choreographer(s) and title(s) of the work(s) you have chosen to discuss. When writing about a specific dancer(s) identify them, when possible.

Dance Critique Pet Peeves:

When writing about the subjects below:

Refer to male dancers, men or danseurs (if classical ballet)

NOT men dancers, boys, guys or males

Refer to female dancers, women or ballerinas (if classical ballet)

NOT women dancers, girls, gals, chicks or females

Refer to a piece, work or dance

NOT routine or act

Refer to movements

NOT moves

Refer to live music

NOT live musicians

Refer to recorded or pre-recorded music

NOT taped music

Refer to danced together or in unison

NOT in sync or synchronized

Refer to the performance or the concert

NOT the show, play or recital

DO use both names ("Catherine Zeta-Jones danced well in *Chicago*" or "Ms. Zeta-Jones danced well in *Chicago*.")

DO NOT use first names only to refer to dancers ("Catherine danced well in *Chicago*")

DO write in the third person

NOT in the first person

DO NOT make general assumptions for the audience

DO NOT include title page information on first page of critique (name, date, professor's name, class, performance)

DO NOT switch tenses;

Example when to alternate tense;

(*Serenade* was performed poorly yet it is a choreographic triumph.)

Example when not to alternate tense;

(On Friday night the dancers **appeared** tired which **causes** the choreography to be lack luster.)

DO NOT identify the performers in a list from the program notes.

(Adapted from http://writing2.richmond.edu/writing/wweb/dance/danceguide.html)

Chapter Eleven

Final Words on Writing a Literary Analysis Paper

The Purpose of a Literary Analysis:

A literary analysis is not merely a summary of a literary work. Instead, it is an argument about the work that expresses a writer's personal perspective, interpretation, judgment, or critical evaluation of the work. This is accomplished by examining the literary devices, word choices, or writing structures the author uses within the work. The purpose of a literary analysis is to demonstrate why the author used specific ideas, word choices, or writing structures to convey his or her message.

How to Create a Literary Analysis?

1. Read the text closely several times. Focus on the ideas that are being presented. Think about the characters' development and the author's writing technique. What might be considered interesting, unusual, or important?

2. Brainstorm a list of potential topics. Highlight important passages in the text and take notes on these passages. Later, when writing the paper, these notes should help a writer to remember which aspects of the story caught his/her attention. The topic chosen should always be based on a writer's interpretation of the author's message. Here are some things a writer may want to consider when brainstorming for a literary analysis.

Character: What observations might a writer make about the characters? Are there discrepancies in what they think, say, or do? Are the observations a writer makes different from what other characters say? How does the author describe the characters? Are the characters "dynamic" (a dynamic character is a character that undergoes important changes throughout the work)? Are the characters "static" characters (a static character is a character that stays the same throughout the work)?

Are the characters "flat" characters (a flat character is a character that does not have vivid character traits) or "round" characters (a round character is a character that has vivid character traits)? Are the characters symbolic or representative of some universal quality? Is it possible that two characters in the text might be compared or contrasted?

Setting: Is there a relationship between the work's setting and its mood? Does the setting reflect the work's theme? How does the setting impact the characters? Does a change in the setting affect the mood, characters, or conflict?

Plot: How might the beginning of the work be interpreted? How does the plot build suspense? Does the author use techniques such as foreshadowing or flashback? Are there patterns of cause-effect relationships? Do events occur in a logical order?

Examine the events that lead to the climax and determine how the work ends?

Theme: What is the major idea or theme of the work? How does the author relay this theme? Is there a greater meaning to the details given? How do the characters' moods affect the theme? What allusions are made throughout the work? Are there repeating patterns or symbols? What does the title say about the theme?

Dialogue: What is the purpose of the dialogue? Is the dialogue appropriate in terms of word choice or sentence length? How does the dialogue impact the characterization? How does the author use the dialogue to show the mood of the characters? How does this aid the author's message? How does the dialogue impact the plot?

Imagery: In what way might a specific image or series of images be analyzed? How might the development of images throughout the work be explained? Are the images important to the meaning of the work? How are images interrelated with other literary elements?

Figures of speech: How are figures of speech such as similes, metaphors, and hyperboles used throughout the text? How are these figures of speech important in relation to the meaning of the text? Are figures of speech interrelated between other literary elements?

Tone: How might describe the attitude of the author or the tone of the work be described? Is the tone serious, playful, casual, formal, or somber? How does the author achieve this tone? How does the tone impact the author's message? Does the author say one thing but mean another? Does the author take the subject seriously or treat it lightly?

Rhyme/Rhythm: Do the author's words, sentences, or paragraphs seem to share a similar rhyme pattern? What type of rhythm does the author seem to be creating?

How is this rhyme/rhythm impacting the author's message? Does the author use the different rhymes/rhythms as a sound device for the literary work? How does the author do this?

Point of View: What point of view do the characters display? First, second, or third?

How does this point of view affect the theme, plot, or conflict of the work? How might the author's point of view impact a writer's analysis? Might the character's first person point of view draws a writer to feel as though he/she is hearing a personal account and cause him/her to feel an intimate connection with the character? Might the author's third person account cause a writer to feel as if the author is acting as the narrator of the story? Or might it cause a writer to believe that the narrator is an omniscient being who is distant but knows the character's thoughts and feelings?

3. Think about what the author is trying to say. Why is this important? When viewing this work as a piece of art, what might a writer's response be? What might a writer's reactions be to the ideas presented in the work? Are these ideas truthful or relevant to today and how? If a writer were asked what they thought of this work how might they respond? What points might a writer make?"

4. Select a topic that has sufficient supporting evidence. A writer should make sure to include specific details to support the topic. Use highlighted sections of the book as evidence to support the topic that has been chosen.

5. Write a working thesis. The analysis will need a strong thesis that states a writer's perspective but also allows it to be debated. The thesis should state a writer's opinion, but it should also allow readers to arrive at their own conclusions.

Example of a **debatable thesis**:

Pride and Prejudice is about Elizabeth Bennett's effort to overcome her own proud behavior and discrimination towards Mr. Darcy, as well as how her family is affected by the haughtiness and preconceptions of the society around them.

(*This is a debatable thesis because it asks the reader, "Does Elizabeth actually exhibit haughtiness and preconceptions? Is this why she doesn't get along with Mr. Darcy? How is Elizabeth's family affected by the haughtiness and preconceptions of the society around them?"*)

Avoid a **non-debatable thesis**:

Example: *Pride and Prejudice* is about five sisters and their journey to find love.

(*This thesis is non-debatable because it is undisputable. The paper is framed as a summary rather than as a literary analysis.*)

6. Make an extended list of evidence. Find more evidence from the text to support the working thesis. Then select the evidence that will be used in the paper.

7. Refine the thesis. Make sure the thesis fits with the evidence that has been presented.

8. Organize the evidence. Match the evidence to the order of the thesis. Delete any of the original textual supports that may no longer follow the thesis, and gather new evidence if needed.

9. Interpret the evidence. When writing a literary analysis, it is very important for writers to make sure they express their own personal interpretation of the work. Be careful that the literary analysis is not a summary.

10. Create a rough draft. When writing a rough draft, there are several methods that may aid a writer in creating a strong final draft.

Here are a few methods:

Outline: An outline will help a writer to organize his/her thoughts and ideas. It will remind a writer of the order of the thesis, as well as the supporting points he/she would like each topic sentence to have.

Free-write: A short, ten minute free-write will help to get all of a writer's thoughts on paper. It will allow a writer to focus on the content, rather than the punctuation and spelling. Once the free-write is complete, a writer can read through it and circle the points that are strong, as well as omit the ones that are not.

Bubble Map: A bubble map will allow a writer to draw connections from one idea to the next. It will give a writer a visual idea of the direction of the literary analysis, as well as help a writer to see the connections between the topics. This can help a writer transition from one topic to another more fluidly.

11. Revise the Analysis. After completing the first draft, revise the analysis by considering the following questions:

F. Is the thesis clearly stated in the first paragraph?

G. Is the sentence structure varied?

H. Does the structure of the analysis emphasize the main ideas?

I. Is the third-person point of view used throughout the entire essay?

J. Has the present tense been used to discuss the work and past tense to describe the author's background?

H. Have quotation marks been used around direct quotations?

I. Have the sources been cited correctly according to MLA style?

J. Has extraneous information that does not support the thesis been eliminated?

K. Have clear transitions been used between sentences and paragraphs?

12. Proofread. Once the content of the essay is well-developed, it should be proofread for grammar, punctuation, and spelling. It is often helpful to read the paper slowly and clearly out loud. If possible, another person should listen and read along as the paper is being read.

The paper should be printed and proofread several times until an accurate final copy is created. Be alert to common grammatical errors such as sentence fragments, comma splices, or run-on sentences. Remember to consult a style manual for grammatical or citation questions, and if further assistance is desired, group workshops and individual appointments are available free of charge through Tutoring Services

Final Words on the Structure for Literary Analysis Essay

I. Get a Catchy Title

II. Paragraph 1: Introduction

A. Hook

B. Author

C. Title

D. Main characters

E. A short summary

F. Thesis

G. Transitional sentence

III. Paragraph 2: First Body Paragraph

A. Topic sentence (what this paragraph will discuss, how it will prove your thesis)

B. Context for the quote

1. Who says it?

2. What's happening in the text when they say it?

C. Quote from the text (cited appropriately)

D. Analysis of the quote: How does it prove your thesis?

E. Closing sentence (wrap up the paragraph to effectively transition to the next paragraph)

IV. Paragraph 3: Second Body Paragraph

A. Topic sentence (what this paragraph will discuss, how it will prove your thesis)

B. Context for the quote

1. Who says it?

2. What's happening in the text when they say it?

C. Quote from the text (cited appropriately)

D. Analysis of the quote: How does it prove your thesis?

E. Closing sentence (wrap up the paragraph to effectively transition to the next paragraph

V. Paragraph 4: Third Body Paragraph

A. Topic sentence (what this paragraph will discuss, how it will prove your thesis)

B. Context for the quote

1. Who says it?

2. What's happening in the text when they say it?

C. Quote from the text (cited appropriately)

D. Analysis of the quote: How does it prove your thesis?

E. Closing sentence (wrap up the paragraph to effectively transition to the next paragraph

VI. Conclusion (You do not necessarily have to follow this order, but include the following):

A. Summarize your argument.

B. Extend the argument.

C. Show why the text is important.

VII. Works Cited

Chapter Twelve

Examples of Literary Terms

When an author sits down to write a story, a song, a poem or a play, he or she does not simply write what happened. Instead, he or she uses what are called literary devices which are narrative techniques that add texture, energy, and excitement to the narrative, grip the reader's imagination, and convey information. While there are literally hundreds of literary devices at an author's disposal, what follows are a handful of the most common. Literary devices or literary techniques are therefore specific structures that writers often use to add meaning or create more compelling stories for the reader. Some common examples are metaphor, alliteration, hyperbole, and imagery. These techniques can give the reader a greater understanding and meaning of the writer's intent.

Allegory

Definition:

An allegory is a symbolism device where the meaning of a greater, often abstract, concept is conveyed with the aid of a more corporeal object or idea being used as an example. Usually a rhetoric device, an allegory suggests a meaning via metaphoric examples.

Example:

Faith is like a stony uphill climb: a single stumble might send you sprawling but belief and steadfastness will see you to the very top.

Alliteration

Definition:

Alliteration is a literary device where words are used in quick succession and begin with letters belonging to the same sound group.

Whether it is the consonant sound or a specific vowel group, the alliteration involves creating a repetition of similar sounds in the sentence. Alliterations are also created when the words all begin with the same letter. Alliterations are used to add character to the writing and often add an element of 'fun' to the piece.

Example:

The Wicked Witch of the West went her own way. (The 'W' sound is highlighted and repeated throughout the sentence.)

Allusion

Definition:

An allusion is a figure of speech whereby the author refers to a subject matter such as a place, event, or literary work by way of a passing reference. It is up to the reader to make a connection to the subject being mentioned.

Example:

It's no wonder everyone refers to Mary as another Mother Teresa in the making; she loves to help and care after people everywhere-from the streets to her own friends.

In the example the author uses the mention of Mother Teresa to indicate the sort of qualities that Mary has.

Amplification

Definition:

Amplification refers to a literary practice wherein the writer embellishes the sentence by adding more information to it in order to increase its worth and understandability. When a plain sentence is too abrupt and fails to convey the full implications desired, amplification comes into play when the writer adds more to the structure to give it more meaning.

Example:

Original sentence- The thesis paper was difficult. After amplification- The thesis paper was difficult: it required extensive research, data collection, sample surveys, interviews and a lot of fieldwork.

Anagram

Definition:

Anagrams are an extremely popular form of literary device wherein the writer jumbles up parts of the word to create a new word. From the syllables of a phrase to the individual letters of a word, any fraction can be jumbled to create a new form. Anagram is a form of wordplay that allows the writer to infuse mystery and a little interactive fun in the writing so that the reader can decipher the actual word on their own and discover a depth of meaning to the writing.

Example:

An anagram for "debit card" is "bad credit". As you can see, both phrases use the same letters. By mixing the letters a bit of humor is created.

Analogy

Definition:

An analogy is a literary device that helps to establish a relationship based on similarities between two concepts or ideas. By using an analogy we can convey a new idea by using the blueprint of an old one as a basis for understanding. With a mental linkage between the two, one can create understanding regarding the new concept in a simple and succinct manner.

Example:

In the same way as one cannot have the rainbow without the rain, one cannot achieve success and riches without hard work.

Anastrophe

Definition:

Anastrophe is a form of literary device wherein the order of the noun and the adjective in the sentence is exchanged. In standard parlance and writing the adjective comes before the noun but when one is employing an anastrophe the noun is followed by the adjective. This reversed order creates a dramatic impact and lends weight to the description offered by the adjective.

Example:

He spoke of times past and future, and dreamt of things to be.

Anecdote

Definition:

The word anecdote, phonetically pronounced "*an.ik.doht,*" means a short verbal accounting of a funny, amusing, interesting event or incident. The story is usually a reminiscence from the teller's life but at best is a related story of fact, as opposed to a contrived work of fiction. The origin of the word anecdote comes from the Greek Byzantine period, A.D. 527 to 565 during the reign of emperor Justinian. In his court, Justinian had a historian named Procopius who was a gifted writer who wrote many witty, amusing and somewhat bawdy accounts of court life. Never intending for this stories to become public he entitled his writings as "Anecdota" which was Greek for unpublished and kept secret. After his secret writings did indeed become public and published, the term anecdote became commonly used for similar accounts.

Example:

Amusing anecdotes many times find their way into wedding receptions, family reunions and any other gathering of people who know each other well. Teachers and educators often tell classrooms of pupils anecdotes about famous people. The anecdotes are not always flattering, but are usually revealing of character and invariably amusing. Here is an example of an anecdote about Winston Churchill:

Winston Churchill was very fond of his pet dog Rufus. He ate in the dining room with the family on a special cloth and was treated with utmost respect. When enjoying movies, Rufus had the best seat in the house; on Winston Churchill's lap. While watching "Oliver Twist," Churchill put his hands over Rufus' eyes during the scene where Bill Sike's intends to drown his dog. Churchill is believed to have said to Rufus: "don't look now, dear. I'll tell you about it later."

Anthropomorphism

Definition:

Anthropomorphism can be understood to be the act of lending a human quality, emotion or ambition to a non-human object or being. This act of lending a human element to a non-human subject is often employed in order to endear the latter to the readers or audience and increase the level of relativity between the two while also lending character to the subject.

Example:

The raging storm brought with it howling winds and fierce lightning as the residents of the village looked up at the angry skies in alarm.

Antithesis

Definition:

An antithesis is used when the writer employs two sentences of contrasting meanings in close proximity to one another. Whether they are words or phrases of the same sentence, an antithesis is used to create a stark contrast using two divergent elements that come together to create one uniform whole. An antithesis plays on the complementary property of opposites to create one vivid picture. The purpose of using an antithesis in literature is to create a balance between opposite qualities and lend a greater insight into the subject.

Example:

When Neil Armstrong walked on the moon it might have been one small step for a man but it was one giant leap for mankind.

Aphorism

Definition:

An aphorism is a concise statement that is made in a matter of fact tone to state a principle or an opinion that is generally understood to be a universal truth. Aphorisms are often adages, wise sayings and maxims aimed at imparting sense and wisdom. It is to be noted that aphorisms are usually witty and curt and often have an underlying tone of authority to them.

Example:

Upon seeing the shoddy work done by the employee the boss told him to "either shape up or ship out".

Archetype

Definition:

An archetype is a reference to a concept, a person or an object that has served as a prototype of its kind and is the original idea that has come to be used over and over again. Archetypes are literary devices that employ the use of a famous concept, person or object to convey a wealth of meaning. Archetypes are immediately identifiable and even though they run the risk of being overused, they are still the best examples of their kind.

Example:

Romeo and Juliet are an archetype of eternal love and a star-crossed love story.

Assonance

Definition:

Assonance refers to repetition of sounds produced by vowels within a sentence or phrase. In this regard assonance can be understood to be a kind of alliteration. What sets it apart from alliterations is that it is the repetition of only vowel sounds. Assonance is the opposite of consonance, which implies repetitive usage of consonant sounds.

Example:

"A long song". (Where the 'o' sound is repeated in the last two words of the sentence)

Asyndeton

Definition:

Asyndeton refers to a practice in literature whereby the author purposely leaves out conjunctions in the sentence, while maintaining the grammatical accuracy of the phrase. Asyndeton as a literary tool helps in shortening up the implied meaning of the entire phrase and presenting it in a succinct form. This compact version helps in creating an immediate impact whereby the reader is instantly attuned to what the writer is trying to convey. Use of this literary device helps in creating a strong impact and such sentences have greater recall worth since the idea is presented in a nutshell.

Example:

1. Read, Write, Learn.

2. Watch, Absorb, Understand.

3. Reduce, Reuse, Recycle.

Authorial Intrusion

Definition:

Authorial Intrusion is an interesting literary device wherein the author penning the story, poem or prose steps away from the text and speaks out to the reader. Authorial Intrusion establishes a one to one relationship between the writer and the reader where the latter is no longer a secondary player or an indirect audience to the progress of the story but is the main subject of the author's attention.

Example:

In many olden novels, especially in suspense novels, the protagonist would move away from the stream of the story and speak out to the reader. This technique was often used to reveal some crucial elements of the story to the reader even though the protagonist might remain mystified within the story for the time being.

Bibliomancy

Definition:

As the very name itself suggests, this kind of literary device finds its roots in biblical origins. This term refers to the practice of basing a plot happening or event and anticipating the results it will have on a faction of the Bible. It involves a random selection process wherein the biblical passage is chosen as a founding stone for basing the outcome of the writing. In an overall context, not limited to just literature, bibliomancy refers to foretelling the future by turning to random portions of the Bible for guidance.

Example:

The Vedas serve as a tool for Bibliomancy to the Hindus while Muslims rely on the Koran.

Bildungsroman

Definition:

This is a very popular form of storytelling whereby the author bases the plot on the overall growth of the central character throughout the timeline of the story. As the story progresses, the subject undergoes noticeable mental, physical, social, emotional, moral, and often spiritual advancement and strengthening before the readers' eyes. It has often been seen that the protagonist begins with views, aims and dreams that are in contrast to the other character's in the story and then fights his or her way through to achieve them.

Example:

Scarlet O'Hara in Gone With the Wind experiences immense personal growth as she learns the value of friends and hard work under duress, without compromising her own dreams.

Cacophony

Definition:

A cacophony in literature refers to the use of words and phrases that imply strong, harsh sounds within the phrase. These words have jarring and dissonant sounds that create a disturbing, objectionable atmosphere.

Example:

His fingers rapped and pounded the door, and his foot thumped against the yellowing wood.

Caesura

Definition:

This literary device involves creating a fracture of sorts within a sentence where the two separate parts are distinguishable from one another yet intrinsically linked to one another. The purpose of using a caesura is to create a dramatic pause, which has a strong impact. The pause helps to add an emotional, often theatrical touch to the sentence and conveys a depth of sentiment in a short phrase.

Example:

Mozart- oh how your music makes me soar!

Characterization

Definition:

Characterization in literature refers the step by step process wherein an author introduces and then describes a character. The character can be described directly by the author or indirectly through the actions, thoughts, and speech of the character.

Example:

Michael Corleone was not jus' a mafiaso, but a family man. A man who walked the knife's edge to preserve his sanity.

Chiasmus

Definition:

Chiasmus is a figure of speech containing two phrases that are parallel but inverted to each other.

Example:

You can take the patriot out of the country but you cannot take the country out of the patriot.

Circumlocution

Definition:

Circumlocution is a form of writing where the writer uses exaggeratedly long and complex sentences in order to convey a meaning that could have otherwise been conveyed through a shorter, much simpler sentence. Circumlocution involves stating an idea or a view in an indirect manner that leaves the reader guessing and grasping at the actual meaning.

Example:

Instead of writing "At 8 pm he arrived by car for the dinner party." the author writes, "Around 3 hours after sunset, it was winter at the time, the man arrived in a combustion engine driven piece of technology with four wheels to join other bipedal creatures in the ingestion of somewhat large quantities of food and drink while having discourse around a large wooden mesa designed for such a purpose".

Conflict

Definition:

It is a literary device used for expressing a resistance the protagonist of the story finds in achieving his aims or dreams. The conflict is a discord that can have external aggressors or can even arise from within the self. It can occur when the subject is battling his inner discord, at odds with his surroundings or it may be pitted against others in the story.

Example:

John tried hard to convince himself that his Hollywood dreams were worth the struggle but his parents, and his inner voice of reason, failed to agree.

Connotation

Definition:

Connotations are the associations people make with words that go beyond the literal or dictionary definition. Many words have connotations that create emotions or feelings in the reader.

Example:

And once again, the autumn leaves were falling.

This phrase uses 'autumn' to signify something coming to an end.

Consonance

Definition:

Consonance refers to repetition of sounds in quick succession produced by consonants within a sentence or phrase. The repetitive sound is often found at the end of a word. Consonance is the opposite of assonance, which implies repetitive usage of vowel sounds.

Example:

He struck a streak of bad luck.

Denotation

Definition:

Denotation refers to the use of the dictionary definition or literal meaning of a word.

Example:

They built a house.

In the above sentence, house is meant literally as in a building where a family lives. If the word "home" was used instead in the above sentence in place of "house", the meaning would not be so literal as there are many emotions associated with the word "home" beyond simply the structure where people live.

Deus-ex-Machina

Definition:

Deus ex Machina is a rather debatable and often criticized form of literary device. It refers to the incidence where an implausible concept or character is brought into the story in order to make the conflict in the story resolve and to bring about a pleasing solution. The use of Deus ex Machina is not recommended as it is seen to be the mark of a poor plot that the writer needs to resort to random, insupportable and unbelievable twists and turns to reach the end of the story.

Example:

If in a suspense novel the protagonist suddenly finds a solution to his dilemmas because of divine intervention.

Diction

Definition:

Diction is the distinctive tone or tenor of an author's writings. Diction is not just a writer's choice of words it can include the mood, attitude, dialect and style of writing. Diction is usually judged with reference to the prevailing standards of proper writing and speech and is seen as the mark of quality of the writing. It is also understood as the selection of certain words or phrases that become peculiar to a writer.

Example:

Certain writers in the modern day and age use archaic terms such as 'thy', 'thee' and 'wherefore' to imbue a Shakespearean mood to their work.

Doppelganger

Definition:

The term is derived from the German language and literally translates into 'double walker'. It refers to a character in the story that is actually a counterfeit or a copy of a genuine character. Doppelgangers of the main characters usually bear the ability to impersonate the original but have vastly different spirits and intentions. The doppelganger usually has a different appearance but an earthly soul and supernatural hoodwinking abilities that allow it to fool other unsuspecting characters.

Example:

Dr. Jekyll and Mr. Hyde

Ekphrastic

Definition:

Ekphrastic refers to a form of writing, mostly poetry, wherein the author describes another work of art, usually visual. It is used to convey the deeper symbolism of the corporeal art form by means of a separate medium. It has often been found that ekphrastic writing is rhetorical in nature and symbolic of a greater meaning.

Example:

A photograph of an empty landscape can convey desolation, abandon and loss. Similarly, one can convey the same sentiments and concepts by using phrases such as 'an empty doorway' or 'a childless nursery'.

Epilogue

Definition:

Epilogues are an inherent part of any story or poem and are essential to the structure of any written form. The epilogue is an important literary tool that acts as the afterword once the last chapter is over. The purpose of an epilogue is to add a little insight to some interesting developments that happen once the major plot is over. Epilogues often act as a teaser trailer to any possible sequels that might be created later. Sometimes the epilogue is used to add a little bit about the life or future of the main characters after the story itself has unfolded and wrapped up. Epilogues can be written in a number of ways: sometimes the same narrative style as adopted in the story is continued while at other times one of the characters might take up the narrative or speak one to one with the audience.

Example:

In a remarkably contemporary moment at the end of The Tempest, Shakespeare's wizard Prospero addresses the audience directly, breaking down the boundaries of the play. He informs them that the play is over, his powers are gone, and thus his escape from the play's island setting depends on their applause that they, in effect, get to decide his fate.

This serves as a Epilogue for Shakespeare's tragi-comedy The Tempest.

Epithet

Definition:

An epithet is a literary device that is used as a descriptive device. It is usually used to add to a person or place's regular name and attribute some special quality to the same. Epithets are remarkable in that they become a part of common parlance over time. These descriptive words and phrases can be used to enhance the persona of real and fictitious places, objects, persons and divinities.

Example:

"Alexander the Great" is the epithet commonly used to refer to Alexander III of Macedon. The young king has come to be recognized by this epithet in all of history and popular culture owing to his spectacular achievements in creating one of the largest ever historical empires.

Euphemism

Definition:

The term 'euphemism' is used to refer to the literary practice of using a comparatively milder or less abrasive form of a negative description instead of its original, unsympathetic form. This device is used when writing about matters such as sex, violence, death, crimes and things "embarrassing". The purpose of euphemisms is to substitute unpleasant and severe words with more genteel ones in order to mask the harshness. The use of euphemisms is sometimes manipulated to lend a touch of exaggeration or irony in satirical writing.

Example:

Using "to put out to pasture" when one implies retiring a person because they are too old to be effective.

Below are some more examples of Euphemisms

Downsizing - This is used when a company fires or lays off a larger number of employees

Friendly fire - This is used by the military when soldiers are accidentally killed by other soldiers on the same side.

Tipsy - This is a soft way to say that someone has had to much to drink.

Golden years - This is used to describe the later period of life when someone is of old age.

Gone to heaven - This is a polite way to say that someone is dead.

Enhanced interrogation - This is modern euphemism to minimize what by many people would be viewed as torture.

Euphony

Definition:

The literary device "euphony" refers to the use of phrases and words that are noted for possessing an extensive degree of notable loveliness or melody in the sound they create. The use of euphony is predominant in literary prose and poetry, where poetic devices such as alliterations, rhymes and assonace are used to create pleasant sounds. Euphony is the opposite of cacophony, which refers to the creation of unpleasant and harsh sounds by using certain words and phrases together. This literary devices is based on the use and manipulation of phonetics in literature.

Example:

It has been said that the phrase "cellar door" is reportedly the most pleasant sounding phrase in the English language. The phrase is said to depict the highest degree of euphony, and is said to be especially notable when spoken in the British accent.

Faulty Parallelism

Definition:

In literature, the term 'parallelism' is used to refer to the practice placing together similarly structure related phrases, words or clauses. Parallelism involves placing sentence items in a parallel grammatical format wherein nouns are listed together, specific verb forms are listed together and the like. When one fails to follow this parallel structure, it results in faulty parallelism. The failure to maintain a balance in grammatical forms is known as faulty parallelism wherein similar grammatical forms receive dissimilar or unequal weight.

Example:

On the TV show The Simpsons, lead character Bart Simpson says, "they are laughing, not with me".

Flashback

Definition:

Flashback is a literary device wherein the author depicts the occurrence of specific events to the reader, which have taken place before the present time the narration is following, or events that have happened before the events that are currently unfolding in the story. Flashback devices that are commonly used are past narratives by characters, depictions and references of dreams and memories and a sub device known as authorial sovereignty wherein the author directly chooses to refer to a past occurrence by bringing it up in a straightforward manner. Flashback is used to create a background to the present situation, place or person.

Example:

Back in the day when Sarah was a young girl...

You can see flashbacks used very often in movies. For example, it is common in movies for there to be a flashback that gives the viewer a look into the characters life when they were younger, or when they have done something previously. This is done to help the viewer better understand the present situation.

Foil

Definition:

A foil is another character in a story who contrasts with the main character, usually to highlight one of their attributes.

Example:

In the popular book series, Harry Potter, the character of Hogwarts principal Albus Dumbledore, who portrays 'good', is constantly shown to believe in the power of true love (of all forms and types) and is portrayed as a strong, benevolent and positive character while the antagonist Lord Voldemort, who depicts the evil and 'bad' in the series is constantly shown to mock and disbelieve the sentiment of love and think of it as a foolish indulgence, a trait that is finally his undoing.

Foreshadowing

Definition:

The literary device foreshadowing refers to the use of indicative word or phrases and hints that set the stage for a story to unfold and give the reader a hint of something that is going to happen without revealing the story or spoiling the suspense. Foreshadowing is used to suggest an upcoming outcome to the story.

Example:

"He had no idea of the disastrous chain of events to follow". In this sentence, while the protagonist is clueless of further developments, the reader learns that something disastrous and problematic is about to happen to/for him.

Hubris

Definition:

Hubris, in this day and age, is another way of saying overly arrogant. You can tell the difference of hubris and just regular arrogance or pride by the fact that the character has seemed to allow reality slip away from them. The character portraying hubris, also commonly referred to as hybris, may have just gained a huge amount of power and the false belief that they are "untouchable". This term hubris used to have a slightly different meaning and was a very negative subject back in ancient Greek. It used to be closely related to a crime in Athens. In writing and literature hubris is generally considered a "tragic flaw" and it is saved for the protagonist. The reason for this is because at the end of the story you should be able to see that it is this flaw that brings the "bad guy" down.

Example:

A classic example of hubris is featured in Shakespeare's play Macbeth. Macbeth, the protagonist, overfilled with ambition and arrogance, allows his hubris to think you would be able to kill the valiant Duncan without penalty so he can claim the throne of Scotland for himself. Obviously murder is highly frowned upon, so this eventually leads to Macbeth's demise as well.

Hyperbaton

Definition:

A hyperbaton is a literary device wherein the author plays with the regular positioning of words and phrases and creates a differently structured sentence to convey the same meaning. It is said that by using a hyperbaton, words or phrases overstep their conventional placements and result in a more complex and intriguing sentence structure. This literary device is used to add more depth and interest to the sentence structure.

Example:

"Alone he walked on the cold, lonely roads". This sentence is a variation of the more conventional, "He walked alone on the cold, lonely roads".

Hyperbole

Definition:

A hyperbole is a literary device wherein the author uses specific words and phrases that exaggerate and overemphasize the basic crux of the statement in order to produce a grander, more noticeable effect. The purpose of hyperbole is to create a larger-than-life effect and overly stress a specific point. Such sentences usually convey an action or sentiment that is generally not practically/ realistically possible or plausible but helps emphasize an emotion.

Example:

"I am so tired I cannot walk another inch" or "I'm so sleepy I might fall asleep standing here".

Imagery

Definition:

In literature, one of the strongest devices is imagery wherein the author uses words and phrases to create "mental images" for the reader. Imagery helps the reader to visualize more realistically the author's writings. The usage of metaphors, allusions, descriptive words and similes amongst other literary forms in order to "tickle" and awaken the readers' sensory perceptions is referred to as imagery. Imagery is not limited to only visual sensations, but also refers to igniting kinesthetic, olfactory, tactile, gustatory, thermal and auditory sensations as well.

Example:

The gushing brook stole its way down the lush green mountains, dotted with tiny flowers in a riot of colors and trees coming alive with gaily chirping birds.

Internal Rhyme

Definition:

In literature the internal rhyme is a practice of forming a rhyme in only one lone line of verse. An internal rhyme is also known as the middle rhyme because it is typically constructed in the middle of a line to rhyme with the bit at the end of the same metrical line.

Example:

The line from the famed poem Ancient Mariner, "We were the first that ever burst".

Inversion

Definition:

The term 'inversion' refers to the practice of changing the conventional placement of words. It is a literary practice typical of the older classical poetry genre. In present day literature it is usually used for the purpose of laying emphasis this literary device is more prevalent in poetry than prose because it helps to arrange the poem in a manner that catches the attention of the reader not only with its content but also with its physical appearance; a result of the peculiar structuring.

Example:

In the much known and read Paradise Lost, Milton wrote:

"Of Man's First Disobedience, and the Fruit

Of that Forbidden Tree, whose mortal taste

Brought Death into the World, and all our woe,

With loss of Eden, till one greater Man

Restore us, and regain the blissful Seat,

Sing Heav'nly Muse. . ."

Irony

Definition:

The use of irony in literature refers to playing around with words such that the meaning implied by a sentence or word is actually different from the literal meaning. Often irony is used to suggest the stark contrast of the literal meaning being put forth. The deeper, real layer of significance is revealed not by the words themselves but the situation and the context in which they are placed.

Example:

Writing a sentence such as, "Oh! What fine luck I have!". The sentence on the surface conveys that the speaker is happy with their luck but actually what they mean is that they are extremely unhappy and dissatisfied with their (bad) luck.

Juxtaposition

Definition:

Juxtaposition is a literary device wherein the author places a person, concept, place, idea or theme parallel to another. The purpose of juxtaposing two directly or indirectly related entities close together in literature is to highlight the contrast between the two and compare them. This literary device is usually used for etching out a character in detail, creating suspense or lending a rhetorical effect.

Example:

In Paradise Lost, Milton has used juxtaposition to draw a parallel between the two protagonists, Satan and God, who he discusses by placing their traits in comparison with one another to highlight their differences.

Kennings

Definition:

The use of Kennings in literature is characteristically related to works in Old English poetry where the author would use a twist of words, figure of speech or magic poetic phrase or a newly created compound sentence or phrase to refer to a person, object, place, action or idea. The use of imagery and indicative, direct and indirect references to substitute the proper, formal name of the subject is known as kennings. The use of kennings was also prevalent in Old Norse and Germanic poetry.

Example:

Kennings are rare in modern day language. Here are a few examples from Beowulf:

Battle-sweat = blood

Sky-candle = sun

Whale-road = ocean

Light-of-battle = sword

Litotes

Definition:

Litotes are figures of rhetoric speech that use an understated statement of an affirmative by using a negative description. Rarely talked about, but commonly used in modern day conversations, litotes are a discreet way of saying something unpleasant without directly using negativity. Sometimes called an ironical understatement and/or an avoidance of a truth which can be either positive or negative. Common examples: "I'm not feeling bad," or "he's definitely not a rocket scientist." The actual meanings are: "I am feeling well," and "he is not smart." Litotes were used frequently in Old English Poetry and Literature, and can be found in the English, Russian, German, Dutch and French languages.

Example:

In everyday conversations in the 21st century, one may hear expressions like:

"not the brightest bulb"

"not a beauty"

"not bad"

"not unfamiliar"

These are all examples of negative litotes that mean the opposite: "a dim bulb, or dumb," "plain in appearance," "good," and "knows very well." Perhaps our society is not trying to be humorous or sarcastic, but kinder?

Sometimes double negatives in literature, music and films create litotes that was not intended; for instance in the Rolling Stones hit "I Can't Get No Satisfaction," actually means "I CAN receive satisfaction."

Perhaps some best description litotes are found in the bible: take for instance, Jeremiah 30:19:

"I will multiply them, and they shall not be few; I will make them honored, and they shall not be small." Correctly interpreted, he is saying "there will be many and they will be great or large."

Malapropism

Definition:

Malapropism in literature refers to the practice of misusing words by substituting words with similar sounding words that have different, often unconnected meanings, and thus creating a situation of confusion, misunderstanding and amusement. Malapropism is used to convey that the speaker or character is flustered, bothered, unaware or confused and as a result cannot employ proper diction. A trick to using malapropism is to ensure that the two words (the original and the substitute) sound similar enough for the reader to catch onto the intended switch and find humor in the result.

Example:

In the play *Much Ado About Nothing*, noted playwright William Shakespeare's character Dogberry says, "Our watch, sir, have indeed comprehended two auspicious persons." Instead, what the character means to say is ""'Our watch, sir, have indeed apprehended two suspicious persons."

Metaphor

Definition:

Metaphors are one of the most extensively used literary devices. A metaphor refers to a meaning or identity ascribed to one subject by way of another. In a metaphor, one subject is implied to be another so as to draw a comparison between their similarities and shared traits. The first subject, which is the focus of the sentences is usually compared to the second subject, which is used to convey a degree of meaning that is used to characterize the first. The purpose of using a metaphor is to take an identity or concept that we understand clearly (second subject) and use it to better understand the lesser known element (the first subject).

Example:

"Henry was a lion on the battlefield". This sentence suggests that Henry fought so valiantly and bravely that he embodied all the personality traits we attribute to the ferocious animal. This sentence implies immediately that Henry was courageous and fearless, much like the King of the Jungle.

Metonymy

Definition:

Metonymy in literature refers to the practice of not using the formal word for an object or subject and instead referring to it by using another word that is intricately linked to the formal name or word. It is the practice of substituting the main word with a word that is closely linked to it.

Example:

When we use the name "Washington D.C" we are talking about the U.S' political hot seat by referring to the political capital of the United States because all the significant political institutions such as the White House, Supreme Court, the U.S. Capitol and many more are located her. The phrase "Washington D.C." is metonymy for the government of the U.S. in this case.

Mood

Definition:

The literary device 'mood' refers to a definitive stance the author adopts in shaping a specific emotional perspective towards the subject of the literary work. It refers to the mental and emotional disposition of the author towards the subject, which in turn lends a particular character or atmosphere to the work. The final tone achieved thus is instrumental in evoking specific, appropriate responses from the reader.

Example:

In Erich Segal's Love Story, the relationship of the two protagonists is handled with such beauty, delicateness and sensitivity that the reader is compelled to feel the trials and tribulations of the characters.

Motif

Definition:

The literary device 'motif' is any element, subject, idea or concept that is constantly present through the entire body of literature. Using a motif refers to the repetition of a specific theme dominating the literary work. Motifs are very noticeable and play a significant role in defining the nature of the story, the course of events and the very fabric of the literary piece.

Example:

In many famed fairytales, the motif of a 'handsome prince' falling in love with a 'damsel in distress' and the two being bothered by a wicked step mother, evil witch or beast and finally conquering all to live 'happily ever after' is a common motif.

Another common motif is the simple, pretty peasant girl or girl from a modest background in fairytales discovering that she is actually a royal or noble by the end of the tale.

Negative Capability

Definition:

The use of negative capability in literature is a concept promoted by poet John Keats, who was of the opinion that literary achievers, especially poets, should be able to come to terms with the fact that some matters might have to be left unsolved and uncertain. Keats was of the opinion that some certainties were best left open to imagination and that the element of doubt and ambiguity added romanticism and specialty to a concept.

Example:

The best references of the use of negative capability in literature would be of Keats' own works, especially poems such as Ode on a Grecian Urn and Ode to a Nightingale.

Nemesis

Definition:

In literature, the use of a nemesis refers to a situation of poetic justice wherein the positive characters are rewarded and the negative characters are penalized. The word also sometimes refers to the character or medium by which this justice is brought about as Nemesis was the patron goddess of vengeance according to classical mythology.

Example:

In the popular book series Harry Potter, the protagonist Harry Potter is the nemesis of the evil Lord Voldemort.

Onomatopoeia

Definition:

The term 'onomatopoeia' refers to words whose very sound is very close to the sound they are meant to depict. In other words, it refers to sound words whose pronunciation to the actual sound they represent.

Example:

Words such as grunt, huff, buzz and snap are words whose pronunciation sounds very similar to the actual sounds these words represent. In literature such words are useful in creating a stronger mental image. For instance, sentences such as "the whispering of the forest trees" or "the hum of a thousand bees" or "the click of the door in the nighttime" create vivid mental images.

Oxymoron

Definition:

Oxymoron is a significant literary device as it allows the author to use contradictory, contrasting concepts placed together in a manner that actually ends up making sense in a strange, and slightly complex manner. An oxymoron is an interesting literary device because it helps to perceive a deeper level of truth and explore different layers of semantics while writing.

Example:

Sometimes we cherish things of **little value**.

He possessed a **cold fire** in his eyes.

Paradox

Definition:

A paradox in literature refers to the use of concepts or ideas that are contradictory to one another, yet, when placed together hold significant value on several levels. The uniqueness of paradoxes lies in the fact that a deeper level of meaning and significance is not revealed at first glance, but when it does crystallize, it provides astonishing insight.

Example:

High walls make not a palace; full coffers make not a king.

Pathetic Fallacy

Definition:

Pathetic fallacy is a type of literary device whereby the author ascribes the human feelings of one or more of his or her characters to nonhuman objects or nature or phenomena. It is a type of personification, and is known to occur more by accident and less on purpose.

Example:

The softly whistling teapot informed him it was time for breakfast.

Periodic Structure

Definition:

In literature, the concept of a periodic structure refers to a particular placement of sentence elements such as the main clause of the sentence and/or its predicate are purposely held off and placed at the end instead of at the beginning or their conventional positions. In such placements, the crux of the sentence's meaning does not become clear to the reader until they reach the last part. While undeniably confusing at first, a periodic structure lends a flair of drama and romanticism to a sentence and is greatly used in poetry.

Example:

Instead of writing, "brokenhearted and forlorn she waited till the end of her days for his return" one may write, "for his return, brokenhearted and forlorn, waited she till the end of her days".

Periphrasis

Definition:

The term 'periphrasis' refers to the use of excessive language and surplus words to convey a meaning that could otherwise be conveyed with fewer words and in more direct a manner. The use of this literary device can be to embellish a sentence, to create a grander effect, to beat around the bush and to draw attention away from the crux of the message being conveyed.

Example:

Instead of simply saying "I am displeased with your behavior", one can say, "the manner in which you have conducted yourself in my presence of late has caused me to feel uncomfortable and has resulted in my feeling disgruntled and disappointed with you".

Personification

Definition:

Personification is one of the most commonly used and recognized literary devices. It refers to the practice of attaching human traits and characteristics with inanimate objects, phenomena and animals.

Example:

"The raging winds"

"The wise owl"

"The warm and comforting fire"

Plot

Definition:

The plot usually refers to the sequence of events and happenings that make up a story. There is usually a pattern, unintended or intentional, that threads the plot together. The plot basically refers to the main outcome and order of the story. There is another kind of plot in literature as well; it refers to the conflict or clash occurring as a part of the story. The conflict usually follows 3 regular formats: a) characters in conflict with one another b) characters in conflict with their surroundings and c) characters in conflict with themselves.

Example:

Many date movies follow a similar simple plot. Boy meets girl, boy loses girl, boy wins girl back in the end.

Point of View

Definition:

Point of view is the manner in which a story is narrated or depicted and who it is that tells the story. Simply put, the point of view determines the angle and perception of the story unfolding, and thus influences the tone in which the story takes place. The point of view is instrumental in manipulating the reader's understanding of the narrative. In a way, the point of view can allow or withhold the reader access into the greater reaches of the story. Two of the most common point of view techniques are the first person, wherein the story is told by the narrator from his or her standpoint and the third person wherein the narrator does not figure in the events of the story and tells the story by referring to all characters and places in the third person with third person pronouns and proper nouns.

Example:

In the popular Lord of the Rings book series, the stories are narrated in the third person and all happenings are described from an "outside the story" point of view. Contrastingly, in the popular teen book series, Princess Diaries, the story is told in the first person, by the protagonist herself.

Polysyndeton

Definition:

Polysyndeton refers to the process of using conjunctions or connecting words frequently in a sentence, placed very close to one another. Opposed to the usual norm of using them sparsely, only where they are technically needed. The use of polysyndetons is primarily for adding dramatic effect as they have a strong rhetorical presence.

Example:

For example:

a) Saying "here and there and everywhere", instead of simply saying "here, there and everywhere".

b) "Marge and Susan and Anne and Daisy and Barry all planned to go for a picnic", instead of "Marge, Susan, Anne, Daisy and Barry…" emphasizes each of the individuals and calls attention to every person one by one instead of assembling them as a group.

Portmanteau

Definition:

In literature, this device refers to the practice of joining together two or more words in order to create an entirely new word. This is often done in order to create a name or word for something by combining the individual characteristics of 2 or more other words.

Example:

1. The word "smog" is a portmanteau that was built combining "fog" and "smoke" and "smog" has the properties of both fog and smoke.

2. Liger= Lion + Tiger= A hybrid of the two feline species, possessing characteristics of both.

Prologue

Definition:

A prologue can be understood to be a sort of introduction to a story that usually sets the tone for the story and acts as a bit of a backgrounder or a "sneak peek" into the story. Prologues are typically a narrative 'spoken' by one of the characters and not from the part of the author.

Example:

1. "The origin of this story is..."

2. "It all began one day when…"

Puns

Definition:

Puns are a very popular literary device wherein a word is used in a manner to suggest two or more possible meanings. This is generally done to the effect of creating humor or irony or wryness. Puns can also refer to words that suggest meanings of similar-sounding words. The trick is to make the reader have an "ah!" moment and discover 2 or more meanings.

Example:

Santa's helpers are known as subordinate Clauses.

See more examples of puns at http://punjokes.com/

Rhyme Scheme

Definition:

The rhyme scheme is the practice of rhyming words placed at the end of the lines in the prose or poetry. Rhyme scheme refers to the order in which particular words rhyme. If the alternate words rhyme, it is an "a-b-a-b" rhyme scheme, which means "a" is the rhyme for the lines 1 and 3 and "b" is the rhyme affected in the lines 2 and 4.

Example:

Roses are red (a)

Violets are blue (b)

Beautiful they all may be (c)

But I love you (b)

The above is an "a-b-c-b" rhyme scheme.

Rhythm & Rhyme

Definition:

The concept of 'rhythm and rhyme' refers to a pattern of rhymes that is created by using words that produce the same, or similar sounds. Rhythm and rhyme together refer to the recurrence of similar sounds in prose and poetry, creating a musical, gentle effect.

Example:

"I am a teapot

Short and stout;

This is my handle

And this is my spout.

When the water's boiling

Hear me shout;

Just lift me up

And pour me out"

Satire

Definition:

The use of satire in literature refers to the practice of making fun of a human weakness or character flaw. The use of satire is often inclusive of a need or decision of correcting or bettering the character that is on the receiving end of the satire. In general, even though satire might be humorous and may "make fun", its purpose is not to entertain and amuse but actually to derive a reaction of contempt from the reader.

Example:

An example of satire in modern popculture is the TV series Southpark that uses satire as it primary medium for drawing attention the flaws in society, especially American society at present. The scripts and writing for the show are an excellent example of satire in written form.

Setting

Definition:

In literature, the word 'setting' is used to identify and establish the time, place and mood of the events of the story. It basically helps in establishing where and when and under what circumstances the story is taking place.

Example:

In the first installment of the Harry Potter series, a large part of the book takes place at the protagonist, Harry's, aunt's and uncle's place, living in the "muggle" (non-magical) world with the "muggle" folks, and Harry is unaware of his magical capabilities and blood. This setting establishes the background that Harry has a non-magical childhood with other "muggle" people and has no clue about his special powers or his parents and is raised much like, actually worse than, regular people, till his 11th birthday.

Simile

Definition:

Similes are one of the most commonly used literary devices; referring to the practice of drawing parallels or comparisons between two unrelated and dissimilar things, people, beings, places and concepts. By using similes a greater degree of meaning and understanding is attached to an otherwise simple sentence. The reader is able to better understand the sentiment the author wishes to convey. Similes are marked by the use of the words 'as' or 'such as' or 'like'.

Example:

He is like a mouse in front of the teacher.

Spoonerism

Definition:

Spoonerism refers to the practice of interchanging the first letters of some words in order to create new words or even to create nonsensical words in order to create a humorous setting. While they are often unintentional and known as a "slip of the tongue", in literature they are welcomed as witty wordplay.

Example:

The phrase "flesh and blood" being spoken as a character as "blesh and flood" in urgency and heightened emotion.

Stanza

Definition:

The term stanza refers to a single, related chunk of lines in poetry. It basically refers to one unit or group of lines, which forms one particular faction in poetry. The most basic kind of stanza is usually 4 lines per group, with the simplest rhyme scheme "a-b-a-b" being followed.

Example:

"The greedy paddy cat,

Chased after the mice;

She got so round and fat,

But it tasted so nice"

Stream of consciousness

Definition:

The phrase 'stream of consciousness' refers to an uninterrupted and unhindered collection and occurrence of thoughts and ideas in the conscious mind. In literature, the phrase refers to the flow of these thoughts, with reference to a particular character's thinking process. This literary device is usually used in order to provide a narrative in the form of the character's thoughts instead of using dialogue or description.

Example:

All writings by Virginia Woolff are a good example of literary stream of consciousness.

"Life is not a series of gig lamps symmetrically arranged; life is a luminous halo, a semi-transparent envelope surrounding us from the beginning of consciousness to the end." The Common Reader (1925)

Suspense

Definition:

Suspense is the intense feeling that an audience goes through while waiting for the outcome of certain events. It basically leaves the reader holding their breath and wanting more information. The amount of intensity in a suspenseful moment is why it is hard to put a book down. Without suspense, a reader would lose interest quickly in any story because there is nothing that is making the reader ask, "What's going to happen next?" In writing, there has to be a series of events that leads to a climax that captivates the audience and makes them tense and anxious to know what is going to happen.

Example:

A cliffhanger is a great way to create suspense. You remember when you were a kid and very excited to watch those Saturday morning shows. You can probably recall the feeling you had at the pit of your stomach when, after about 25 minutes and lots of commercials, you were hoping to find out what happened to your favorite character. However, you didn't get to find out. Instead they would make the "Tune In Next Week" announcement and you already knew that you would be there. Same time, same place. Suspense is a powerful literary tool because, if done correctly, you know your audience will be back for more and more.

Symbol

Definition:

A symbol is literary device that contains several layers of meaning, often concealed at first sight, and is representative of several other aspects, concepts or traits than those that are visible in the literal translation alone. Symbol is using an object or action that means something more than its literal meaning.

Example:

The phrase "a new dawn" does not talk only about the actual beginning of a new day but also signifies a new start, a fresh chance to begin and the end of a previous tiring time.

Synecdoche

Definition:

A synecdoche is a literary device that uses a part of something to refer to the whole or vice versa. It is somewhat rhetorical in nature, where the entire object is represented by way of a fraction of it or a fraction of the object is symbolized by the whole.

Example:

"Weary feet in the walk of life", does not refer to the feet actually being tired or painful; it is symbolic of a long, hard struggle through the journey of life and feeling low, tired, unoptimistic and 'the walk of life' does not represent an actual path or distance covered, instead refers to the entire sequence of life events that has made the person tired.

Synesthesia

Definition:

While the term synesthesia literally refers to a medical condition wherein one or many of the sensory modalities become joined to one another, in literature it refers to the depiction of a strong connection, link or bond between the different senses. Characters in literature are sometimes described to be experiences synesthesia. Synesthesia is the conflation of the senses.

Example:

The Sound of Blue by Hollu Payne which portrays synesthesia with respect to the Romantic ideal.

Syntax

Definition:

Syntax in literature refers to the actual way in which words and sentences are placed together in the writing. Usually in the English language the syntax should follow a pattern of subject-verb-object agreement but sometimes authors play around with this to achieve a lyrical, rhythmic, rhetoric or questioning effect. It is not related to the act of choosing specific words or even the meaning of each word or the overall meanings conveyed by the sentences.

Example:

The sentence “The man drives the car” would follow normal syntax in the English language. By changing the syntax to “The car drives the man”, the sentence becomes awkward.

Theme

Definition:

The theme of any literary work is the base that acts as a foundation for the entire literary piece. The theme links all aspects of the literary work with one another and is basically the main subject. The theme can be an enduring pattern or motif throughout the literary work, occurring in a complex, long winding manner or it can be short and succinct and provide a certain insight into the story.

Example:

The main theme in the play Romeo and Juliet was love with smaller themes of sacrifice, tragedy, struggle, hardship, devotion and so on.

Tone

Definition:

The tone of a literary work is the perspective or attitude that the author adopts with regards to a specific character, place or development. Tone can portray a variety of emotions ranging from solemn, grave, and critical to witty, wry and humorous. Tone helps the reader ascertain the writer's feelings towards a particular topic and this in turn influences the reader's understanding of the story.

Example:

In her Harry Potter series, author J.K. Rowling has taken an extremely positive, inspiring and uplifting tone towards the idea of love and devotion.

Tragedy

Definition:

In literature, the concept of tragedy refers to a series of unfortunate events by which one or more of the literary characters in the story undergo several misfortunes, which finally culminate into a disaster of 'epic proportions'. Tragedy is generally built up in 5 stages: a) happy times b) the introduction of a problem c) the problem worsens to a crisis or dilemma d) the characters are unable to prevent the problem from taking over e) the problem results in some catastrophic, grave ending, which is the tragedy culminated.

Example:

In the play Julius Caesar, the lead character is an ambitious, fearless and power hungry king who ignores all the signs and does not heed the advice of the well-meaning: finally being stabbed to death by his own best friend and advisor Brutus. This moment has been immortalized by the phrase "Et tu Brute?", wherein Caesar realizes that he has finally been defeated, and that too through betrayal.

Understatement

Definition:

This literary device refers to the practice of drawing attention to a fact that is already obvious and noticeable. Understating a fact is usually done by way of sarcasm, irony, wryness or any other form of dry humor. Understating something is akin to exaggerating its obviousness as a means of humor.

Example:

The phrase "Oh! I wonder if he could get any later; I am free all day long". Said in a sarcastic tone it indicates that the speaker obviously means the opposite of the literal meaning.

Verisimilitude

Definition:

Verisimilitude tends to be based around the appearance or proximity to being real, or the truth. It was a large part of the work of Karl Popper, and can be used in a variety of different ways to describe something, as well. It is a way of implying the believability or likelihood of a theory or narrative. However, just because something can be described as having Verisimilitude does not mean that it is true, only that merely appears to or seems to be true.

Example:

It can be used in a variety of ways, for example;

"While some dislike the content of the novel due to its graphic nature, you cannot deny that the content certainly gives the book some Verisimilitude"

An example of Verisimilitude in concept, though, could be a doubtful statement in a court of law or even a false testimonial for a restaurant. If something "seems" like it's all well and good, but you can't quite decide, then it can be said to have Verisimilitude.

Verse

Definition:

The literary term 'verse' is used to refer to any single, lone line of a poetry composition. A metrical writing line is known as verse. The word can however, also refer to a stanza or any other part of the poetry.

Example:

A single line or stanza in a poem would be an example of verse.

(Source: http://literary-devices.com/frontpage?page=8)

Chapter Thirteen

Literary Analysis Paper-Rubrics

When writing a literary analysis paper whether it is poetry or prose, your paper must have a thesis which you argue and support throughout your paper with your own ideas and assertions, secondary scholarly sources, and support from the text (examples and quotes).

TS = topic sentence (argumentative statement making a point in support of thesis)

CD = concrete detail (quotes)

CM = commentary (interpretation, explanation of the deeper significance of the quote, proves *how* the topic sentence — and thus, the thesis — are valid)

What is a literary analysis?

In a literary analysis, you write a formal paper in which you make an argument and support your argument with examples from and analysis of a literary text.

A. What is the point?

1. You should be developing your abilities to READ a text, make an ARGUMENT, LOGICALLY support that argument with evidence from the text, write in an ORGANIZED manner which will aid in conveying your points to the reader, and communicate via the written page. The importance of such skills should be obvious.

2. TO MAKE YOU THINK!!!

B. What a literary analysis <u>IS NOT</u>!

1. A paper exploring the relevance of the story to your own life. While your own experience will of course shape your writing style as

well as the story you pick, you should not focus on personal life experiences or use them as arguments for your topic.

2. A summary of the story.

3. A summary of the class notes.

Steps you should take:

1. Formulate a clear Topic Sentence and a Thesis.

2. Formulate a few questions relevant to your thesis which will help you when you reread the story or poem.

3. Reread the story or poem you want to address carefully. Underline passages which are relevant or copy them into your notes. Try to answer the questions you've formulated.

4. Brainstorm ideas: what arguments can you make? What connections come to mind?

5. Reexamine your thesis. Is it supportable? Is it complex enough? Is it interesting?

6. Organize your examples and your ideas. Make a rough outline, including examples and page numbers.

7. Write!

8. Ask yourself: Do my sentences connect? Do my paragraphs connect? (In other words, does this make any sense at all?)

9. Rewrite!

10. Have some else proof read it.

11. Rewrite!

12. Turn in final draft.

Basic Rules for Writing a Literary Analysis

1. Write in the present tense.

- **EXAMPLE:** In Faulkner's "A Rose for Emily," the townspeople **visit** Emily Grierson's house because it **smells** bad.

- **NOT:** In Faulkner's "A Rose for Emily," the townspeople **visited** Emily Grierson's house because it **smelled** bad.

2. Normally, keep yourself out of your analysis; in other words, use the third person (no I or you).

- **FIRST PERSON: I** believe that the narrator in "Sonny's Blues" is a dynamic character because **I** read many details about the changes in his attitude toward and relationship with Sonny.

- **THIRD PERSON: The narrator** in "Sonny's Blues" is a dynamic character **who** changes his attitude toward and relationship with Sonny as the story progresses.

- **SECOND PERSON:** At the end of "Everyday Use," Mama realizes that Maggie is like her but has not received the attention **you** should give **your** daughter to help her attain self-esteem.

- **THIRD PERSON:** At the end of "Everyday Use," Mama realizes that Maggie is like her but has not received enough attention to build self-esteem.

3. Avoid summarizing the plot (i.e., retelling the story literally). Instead analyze (form a thesis about and explain) the story in literary terms.

- **PLOT SUMMARY:** In Edgar Allan Poe's "The Tell-Tale Heart," the mad narrator explains in detail how he kills the old man, who screams as he dies. After being alerted by a neighbor, the police arrive, and the madman gives them a tour through the house, finally halting in the old man's bedroom, where he has buried the man beneath the floor planks under the bed. As he is talking, the narrator hears what he thinks is the old man's heart beating loudly, and he is driven to confess the murder.

- **ANALYSIS:** Though the narrator claims he is not mad, the reader realizes that the narrator in "The Telltale Heart" is unreliable and lies about his sanity. For example, the mad narrator says he can hear "all things in the heaven and in the earth." Sane people cannot. He also lies to the police when he tells them that the shriek they hear occurs in his dream. Though sane people do lie, most do not meticulously plan murders, lie to the police, and then confess without prompting. Finally, the madman is so plagued with guilt that he hears his own conscience in the form of the old man's heart beating loudly. Dead hearts do not beat, nor do sane people confuse their consciences with the sounds of external objects.

- **Include a clear thesis statement which addresses something meaningful about the literature, often about the theme.**

5. Use literary terms to discuss your points (i.e., character, theme, setting, rhyme, point of view, alliteration, symbols, imagery, figurative language, protagonist, and so forth).

- **NONLITERARY TERMS:** To show that women are important, Adrienne Rich writes about Aunt Jennifer and the tigers that she creates in her needlework.

- **LITERARY TERMS:** The poem "Aunt Jennifer's Tigers" contains vivid **images** and **symbols** which reveal a **feminist perspective**.

6. Do not confuse characters' (in fiction or drama) or speakers' (in poetry) viewpoints with authors' viewpoints.

- **AUTHOR:** As a black woman, **Eudora Welty** faces racism in "A Worn Path." (Eudora Welty, the author, was not black.)

- **CHARACTER:** As a black woman, **Old Phoenix** faces racism in "A Worn Path." (Old Phoenix, a character, is black.)

• **POET:** In "Stopping by Woods on a Snowy Evening," **Robert Frost** is tempted to drift into his subconscious dream world, yet he knows he has other obligations to fulfill when he states, "But I have promises to keep, / And miles to go before I sleep." (The pronoun "I" refers to the speaker of the poem, not to Robert Frost, the poet.)

• **SPEAKER:** In "Stopping by Woods on a Snowy Evening," the speaker is tempted to drift into his subconscious dream world, yet he knows he has other obligations to fulfill when he states, "But I have promises to keep, / And miles to go before I sleep." (Here the "I" correctly refers to the speaker of the poem.)

7. Support your points with many quotations and paraphrases, but write the majority of your paper in your own words with your own ideas.

9. Cite prose, poetry, drama, critics, and any other sources used according to specialized MLA standards.

Final Guidelines in Writing a Literary Analysis

1. Write in the present tense.

• **EXAMPLE:** In Faulkner's "A Rose for Emily," the townspeople **visit** Emily Grierson's house because it **smells** bad.

• **NOT:** In Faulkner's "A Rose for Emily," the townspeople **visited** Emily Grierson's house because it **smelled** bad.

2. Normally, keep yourself out of your analysis; in other words, use the third person (no <u>I</u> or <u>you</u>).

• **FIRST PERSON: I** believe that the narrator in "Sonny's Blues" is a dynamic character because **I** read many details about the changes in his attitude toward and relationship with Sonny.

• **THIRD PERSON: The narrator** in "Sonny's Blues" is a dynamic character **who** changes his attitude toward and relationship with Sonny as the story progresses.

- **SECOND PERSON:** At the end of "Everyday Use," Mama realizes that Maggie is like her but has not received the attention **you** should give **your** daughter to help her attain self-esteem.

- **THIRD PERSON:** At the end of "Everyday Use," Mama realizes that Maggie is like her but has not received enough attention to build self-esteem.

3. Avoid summarizing the plot (i.e., retelling the story literally). Instead, analyze (form a thesis about and explain) the story in literary terms.

- **PLOT SUMMARY:** In Edgar Allan Poe's "The Tell-Tale Heart," the mad narrator explains in detail how he kills the old man, who screams as he dies. After being alerted by a neighbor, the police arrive, and the madman gives them a tour through the house, finally halting in the old man's bedroom, where he has buried the man beneath the floor planks under the bed. As he is talking, the narrator hears what he thinks is the old man's heart beating loudly, and he is driven to confess the murder.

- **ANALYSIS:** Though the narrator claims he is not mad, the reader realizes that the narrator in "The Telltale Heart" is unreliable and lies about his sanity. For example, the mad narrator says he can hear "all things in the heaven and in the earth." Sane people cannot. He also lies to the police when he tells them that the shriek they hear occurs in his dream. Though sane people do lie, most do not meticulously plan murders, lie to the police, and then confess without prompting. Finally, the madman is so plagued with guilt that he hears his own conscience in the form of the old man's heart beating loudly. Dead hearts do not beat, nor do sane people confuse their consciences with the sounds of external objects.

4. Include a clear thesis statement which addresses something meaningful about the literature, often about the theme.

5. Use literary terms to discuss your points (i.e., character, theme, setting, rhyme, point of view, alliteration, symbols, imagery, figurative language, protagonist, and so forth).

- **NONLITERARY TERMS:** To show that women are important, Adrienne Rich writes about Aunt Jennifer and the tigers that she creates in her needlework.

- **LITERARY TERMS:** The poem "Aunt Jennifer's Tigers" contains vivid **images** and **symbols** which reveal a **feminist perspective**.

6. Do not confuse characters' (in fiction or drama) or speakers' (in poetry) viewpoints with authors' viewpoints.

- **AUTHOR:** As a black woman, **Eudora Welty** faces racism in "A Worn Path." (Eudora Welty, the author, was not black.)

- **CHARACTER:** As a black woman, **Old Phoenix** faces racism in "A Worn Path." (Old Phoenix, a character, is black.)

- **POET:** In "Stopping by Woods on a Snowy Evening," **Robert Frost** is tempted to drift into his subconscious dream world, yet he knows he has other obligations to fulfill when he states, "But I have promises to keep, / And miles to go before I sleep." (The pronoun "I" refers to the speaker of the poem, not to Robert Frost, the poet.)

- **SPEAKER:** In "Stopping by Woods on a Snowy Evening," the speaker is tempted to drift into his subconscious dream world, yet he knows he has other obligations to fulfill when he states, "But I have promises to keep, / And miles to go before I sleep." (Here the "I" correctly refers to the speaker of the poem.)

7. Support your points with many quotations and paraphrases, but write the majority of your paper in your own words with your own ideas.

8. Cite prose, poetry, drama, critics, and any other sources used according to specialized MLA standards.

Literary Analysis Essay Rubric (Sample)

CATEGORY	4 (6-8 points)	3 (4-6)	2 (2-4)	1 (0-2)	Score
Introduction and Thesis	First paragraph is catchy. Thesis is evident and point to be argued well stated.	First paragraph has a weak "grabber." Thesis is mixed among many sentences and hard to piece together.	A catchy beginning was attempted but was confusing rather than catchy. Thesis is not entirely apparent although topic is evident.	No attempt was made to catch the reader's attention in the first paragraph. Thesis is not apparent nor is the topic of the essay.	___
Quotes and Support	All facts/quotes presented in the essay are accurate and support/relate back to the thesis/topic sentence. 5 quotes present.	Almost all facts/quotes presented in the essay are accurate and occasionally support/relate back to the thesis/topic sentence. 4-5 quotes present.	Most facts/quotes presented in the story are accurate. Evidence is scattered and difficult to follow rather than used to prove your thesis/topic sentence. 3-4 quotes present.	There are several factual/quotation errors in the essay. There is no real effort to make the piece cohesive. 3 or less quotes present.	___
Organization	The essay is very well organized. Five paragraphs (or more) evident. One idea or argument follows another in a logical sequence with clear transitions.	The essay is pretty well organized. Five paragraphs evident. One idea may seem out of place. Clear transitions are used.	The essay is a little hard to follow. Paragraphs are unclear. The transitions are sometimes not clear.	Ideas seem to be randomly arranged. No effort at paragraph organization.	___
Analysis	The essay thoroughly analyzes the author's style/ techniques using literary terms.	The essay analyzes the author's style/ techniques mostly using literary terms.	The essay somewhat analyzes the author's style/ techniques using literary terms, but contains some summary of the plot.	The essay does not analyze the author's style/ techniques using literary terms, or the essay contains little analysis and mostly just summarizes the plot.	___

Closing Paragraph	Conclusion concisely restates thesis statement, main points, and includes an insightful final concluding thought on the topic.	Conclusion restates thesis statement, main points, and includes a final concluding thought on the topic.	Conclusion vaguely restates thesis statement, main points, and includes a weak final unoriginal final thought.	Paper does not contain a conclusion or conclusion is not apparent to reader.	_____
Mechanics	The essay is free of mechanical errors.	The essay has two or three mechanical errors.	The essay has four or five mechanical errors.	The essay has more than five mechanical errors.	_____

Student______________________________Class___________Total Points_____ Letter Grade_____

* Extra 2 pts for legibility

Works Cited

Aaron, J. E. *The Little, Brown Compact Handbook.* 9th Ed. New York: Longman. 2015. Print.

Alzheimer-Europe.org. "The Four Main Approaches." 2009. http://www.alzheimer-europe.org/Research/Understanding-dementia-research/Types-of-research/The-four-main-approaches. 28 June 2014. Web.

Anastas, Jeane W. *Research Design for Social Work and the Human Services.* Chapter 4, Flexible Methods: Case Study Design. 2nd Ed. New York: Columbia University Press, 1999. Print.

Atkinson, Paul and Martyn Hammersley. "Ethnography and Participant Observation." In *Handbook of Qualitative Research.* Norman K. Denzin and Yvonna S. Lincoln, Eds. Thousand Oaks, CA: Sage, pp. 248-261. 1994. Print.

Bachman, Ronet. *The Practice of Research in Criminology and Criminal Justice.* Chapter 5, Causation and Research Designs. 3rd ed. Thousand Oaks, CA: Pine Forge Press, 2007. Print.

Bedford/St. Martin's. "Research and Documentation Online." Fifth Edition. 22 November 2014. Web http://bcs.bedfordstmartins.com/resdoc5e/RES5e_ch08_s1-0001.html

Best, W. John. *Research in Education*, 2nd ed., (Englewood Cliffs, NJ: Prentice-Hall. 1970. Print

Booth, W. C., Colomb, G. C., & Williams, J. M. (1995). The Craft of Research. Chicago: University of Chicago Press. 2001. Print

Bordage G, Dawson B. "Experimental study design and grant writing in 8 steps and 28 questions." *Medical Education*; 37:376–85. 2003. Print.

Bovaird, James A. and Kevin A. Kupzyk. "Sequential Design." In *Encyclopedia of Research Design*. Neil J. Salkind, Ed. Thousand Oaks, CA: Sage, 2010. Print.

Boyce, C. and Neale, P. *Conducting In-depth interviews: A Guide for Designing and Conducting In-depth Interviews for Evaluation Input*. 2006. 29 June 2012. Web.

Bryman, A. *Social Research Methods*. Third Edition. Oxford, UK: Oxford University Press. 2008. Print

Bucknell University. "Developing a Research Topic." https://www.bucknell.edu/Documents/ISR/topic.pdf. JZ 2007

Burley-Allen, M. *Listening: The Forgotten Skill (A self-teaching guide)*. Hoboken, NJ: John Wiley & Sons. 1995. Print

Buzan, T. *The Mind Map Book.* 2 Ed. London, UK: BBC Books. 1995. Print.

CLRC Writing Center. "Structure of a Personal Narrative Essay." Santa Barbara Community College. 16 June 2012 https://www.sbcc.edu/clrc/files/wl/downloads/StructureofaPersonalNarrativeEssay.pdf. Web.

Cooper, Harris, Larry V. Hedges, and Jeffrey C. Valentine, eds. *The Handbook of Research Synthesis and Meta-Analysis*. 2nd edition. New York: Russell Sage Foundation, 2009. Print.

Cornell University Library PSEC Documentation Committee. "APA Citation Style" November 2002; Revised April 2011. https://www.library.cornell.edu/research/citation/apa. 2 November 2013. Web.

Cousin, G. *Researching learning in Higher Education*, Routledge: New York. 2009. Print

Cresswell, J. W. *Research Design: Qualitative, Quantitative, and Mixed methods Approaches*. 2nd ed. Boston: McGraw-Hill. 2000. Print.

Cresswell, John W. "Advanced Mixed-Methods Research Designs." In *Handbook of Mixed Methods in Social and Behavioral Research.* Abbas Tashakkori and Charles Teddle, Eds. Thousand Oaks, CA: Sage. 2003. Print.

Creswell, J. *Qualitative Inquiry and Research Design: Choosing Among Five Approaches*. London: SAGE. 2007. Print.

Danya International, Inc. "The Relationship Between the Research Question, Hypotheses, Specific Aims, and Long-Term Goals of the Project." 2005. Accessed 20 February 2014. http://www.theresearchassistant.com/tutorial/2-1.asp. Web.

David Bordwell and Kristin Thompson, *Film Art*, 6th Ed. McGraw-Hill. 2012. Print

De Vaus, D. A. *Research Design in Social Research.* London: SAGE, 2001

Donoghue, P.J. & Siegel, M.E. *Are You Really Listening? Keys to Successful Communication.* Notre Dame, IN: Sorin Books. 2005. Print

Explorable Psycholgy Experiments. "What is a Literature Review." https://explorable.com/what-is-a-literature-review. Web.

Fink, Arlene. *Conducting Research Literature Reviews: From the Internet to Paper*. 2nd ed. Thousand Oaks, CA: Sage, 2005. Print.

Friesen, B. *Designing and Conducting Your First Interview Project.* San Francisco: Jossey-Bass. 2010. Print.

Gall, Meredith. *Educational Research: An Introduction.* Chapter 18, Action Research. 8th ed. Boston, MA: Pearson/Allyn and Bacon, 2007. Print.

Gibbs, R. W. "Identifying and appreciating poetic metaphor." In *Journal of Literary Semantics* 31, 101-112. 2002. Print

Glatthonr, Allan A. *Writing the Winning Dissertation: A Step-by-Step Guide*. Thousand Oaks, CA: Corwin. 1998. Print.

Glen, Nicole J., "Writing in Elementary School Science: Factors that Influence Teacher Beliefs and Practices." *Teaching and Leadership - Dissertations*. Paper 17. http://surface.syr.edu/tl_etd/17 2008. Web. 12 June 2016.

Goldberg, M. "Some suggestions on 'how to read a film'" 9/14/00 https://faculty.washington.edu/mlg/students/readafilm.htm.

Goldberg, Michael. "Basic Ground Rules of Film Interpretation" https://faculty.washington.edu/mlg/courses/349/349groundrules.htm 12 November 2013. Web.

Hacker, D. *A Writer's Reference*. Boston: Bedford/St. Martin's. 2003. Print.

Hairston, Maxine, and Michael Keene. *Successful Writing*. 5th ed. New York: Norton, 2003. Print

Hall, John. "Cross-Sectional Survey Design." In *Encyclopedia of Survey Research Methods*. Paul J. Lavrakas, ed. (Thousand Oaks, CA: Sage, pp. 173-174. 2008. Print.

Hart, Chris. *Doing a Literature Review: Releasing the Social Science Research Imagination*. Thousand Oaks, CA: Sage Publications, 1998. Print

Healy P, Devane D. "Methodological Considerations in Cohort Study Designs." *Nurse Researcher* 18: 32-36. 2011. Print.

HEFCE, HEFCW, SFC, and DfEL. *Generic Statement on criteria and working methods*. From http://www.rae.ac.uk/pubs/2006/01/docs/genstate.pdf. 2006. [accessed 9 July 2013]. Web.

Hulley S, Cummings S, Browner W, et al. *Designing clinical research*. 3rd ed. Philadelphia (PA): Lippincott Williams and Wilkins; 2007. Print.

Inspiration Software. "Teaching and Learning with Concept Maps." 2014. http://www.inspiration.com/visual-learning/concept-mapping 12 November 2014. Web.

Institute for Writing and Rhetoric, Dartmouth College. "How to Structure and Organize the Research Paper." 2013 http://www.dartmouth.edu/~writing/materials/student/ac_paper/write.shtml. November 08 2014. Web

Jacobs, Christopher P. "Film Theory and Approaches to Criticism or What did That Movie *Mean*?" Spring, 2013. http://www.und.edu/instruct/cjacobs/FilmTheory&Analysis.htm 12 December 2013. Web. 12 April 2015.

Jesson, Jill. *Doing Your Literature Review: Traditional and Systematic Techniques*. London: SAGE, 2011. Print.

Jonassen, D.H., Beissner, K., & Yacci, M.A. *Structural knowledge: Techniques for conveying, assessing, and acquiring structural knowledge*. Hillsdale, NJ: Lawrence Erlbaum Associates. 1993. Print.

Kemmis, Stephen and Robin McTaggart. "Participatory Action Research." In *Handbook of Qualitative Research*. Norman Denzin and Yvonna S. Lincoln, eds. 2nd ed. Thousand Oaks, CA: SAGE, pp. 567-605. 2000. Print.

Kvale, S. *Interviews: An Introduction to Qualitative Research Interviewing*. Thousand Oaks, CA: Sage. 1996. Print

Labaree, Robert V. and Ross Scimeca. "The Philosophical Problem of Truth in Librarianship." *The Library Quarterly* 78:43-70. January 2008. Print

Lakoff, G. "The contemporary theory of metaphor." In: A. Ortony (ed.), *Metaphor and thought. 2nd Edition.* Camb-ridge: Cambridge University Press. 1993. Print.

Lakoff, G. and M. Johnson. *Metaphors we live by*. Chicago: Chicago University Press. 1980. Print

Lanham, R. *Revising Prose*. 4th Ed. New York: Longman. 2000. Print.

Lawson, M. J. "Concept Mapping." In T. Husén & T. N. Postlethwaite (Eds.), *The international encyclopedia of education* (2nd ed., Vol. 2, pp. 1026-1031). Oxford: Elsevier Science. 1994. Print.

Lay, M. M., Wahlstrom, B. J., Rude, C. D., Selfe, C. L, & Selzer, J. *Technical Communication*. 2nd ed. Boston: McGraw-Hill. 2000. Print.

Levin, Kate Ann. "Study Design IV: Cohort Studies." *Evidence-Based Dentistry* 7: 51–52. 2003. Print

Lincoln, Y.S., & Guba, E.G. *Naturalistic Inquiry*. Newbury Park, CA: Sage Publications. 1985. Print.

Lipowski, E. Earlene. "Developing Great Research Questions." *Am J Health-Syst Pharm—Vol 65, 2008.* Sep 1, 2008. Web.

Literature Review Handout. Online Writing Center. Liberty University. http://www.liberty.edu/media/2030/Literature_Review_Handout_Final.pdf. Web.

Locke, L. F., Spirduso, W. W., & Silverman, S. J. *Proposals that Work: A Guide for Planning Dissertations and Grant Proposals*. 4th ed. Thousand Oaks: SAGE. 2000. Print.

Longsfield, Kim. *In-depth Interviews*. http://www.aidsmark.org/ipc_en/pdf/manual/14_Research-Toolkit-Ch6-In-Depth-Interviews.pdf [29 June 2012]. 11 October 2013. Web.

Mack, N., Woodsong, C., MacQueen, K., Guest, G., & Namey, E. *Qualitative Research Methods: A Data Collector's Field Guide*. 2005. http://www.fhi.org/en/RH/Pubs/booksReports/QRM_datacoll.htm 12 October 2013. Web.

Marshall, C., & Rossman, G. B. *Designing Qualitative Research.* 3rd ed. Thousand Oaks, SAGE. 1999. Print.

Maykut, Pamela S. *Beginning Qualitative Research: A Philosophic and Practical Guide.* Washington, D.C.: Falmer Press, 1994; *Stanford Encyclopedia of Philosophy.* Metaphysics Research Lab, CSLI, Stanford University, 2013. Print.

Metz , Christian. *Film Language: A Semiotics of the Cinema.* Chicago: University Of Chicago Press. 1990 Print.

McGraw Hill Higher Education. "Writing a Film Analysis." 7/23/03 highered.mheducation.com/sites/dl/free/.../87183/bog56269_app.pdf. 12 October 2013. Web.

Monaco, James. *How to Read a Film: The Art, Technology, Language, History, and Theory of Film and Media.* Revised Edition. Oxford U. Press: 1981. Print.

Multiprofessional Faculty Development. "What is Educational Research." 2012. Accessed 10 April 2014 http://www.faculty.londondeanery.ac.uk/. Web.

Murray, T. R. *Blending Qualitative and Quantitative Research Methods in Theses and Dissertations.* Thousand Oaks: Corwin. 2003. Print

National Education Association. "Awareness of Education Research Methods: A Guide to Resources: Understanding Validity in Education Research" 2007. http://www.nea.org/home/awareness-of-education-research-methods.htm May 24, 2014. Web.

Nicholas, Tim. *"David Bordwell Shows How Critics Make Meaning Out of Films." 2014.* http://www.partiallyexaminedlife.com/author/tim-nicholas/. 11 September 2013. Web.

Novak, J. D. & A. J. Cañas, "The Theory Underlying Concept Maps and How to Construct Them." 2008. http://cmap.ihmc.us/Publications/ResearchPapers/TheoryUnderlyingConceptMaps.pdf. 11 September 2013. Web

Novak, J. D. How do we learn our lesson? : Taking students through the process. *The Science Teacher, 60*(3), 50-55. 1993. Print.

Novak, J.D. Clarify with concept maps: A tool for students and teachers alike. *The Science Teacher, 58*(7), 45-49. 1991. Print.

Parsell, G and Bligh, J. "The development of a questionnaire to assess the readiness of health care students for interprofessional learning (RIPLS)." *Med Educ.* 1999 Feb; 33(2):95-100. http://www.ncbi.nlm.nih.gov/pubmed/10211258 [accessed 9 October 2014]. [accessed 12 October 2014]. Web.

Penrose, A. M., & Katz, S. B. *Writing in the Sciences: Exploring Conventions of Scientific Discourse*. Boston: Bedford/St. Martin's. 1998. Print.

Punch, K. F. *Developing Effective Research Proposals*. London: SAGE. 2000. Print.

Queensland University of Technology. "Writing a critique." Brisbane, Queensland. 07-Oct-2014. 12 December 2013. http://www.citewrite.qut.edu.au/write/critique.jsp Web.

Quinn Pattern, M. "What is educational research?" *Qualitative Research and Evaluation Methods*. London: SAGE. http://www.faculty.londondeanery.ac.uk/e-learning/introduction-to educational-research/what-is-educational-research. 2002. [accessed 9 July 2013] Web.

Quintero, Esther. "The Data-Driven Education Movement." Shanker Blog: The Voice of the Albert Shanker Institute. Oct. 22, 2012. http://shankerblog.org/?p=7015 [accessed 9 November 2014]. Web.

Reason, Peter and Hilary Bradbury. *Handbook of Action Research: Participative Inquiry and Practice*. Thousand Oaks, CA: SAGE, 2001. Print.

Research Station: Project Design. http://www.nwf.org/campus-ecology/get-involved/design-a-project/design-a-project.aspx

Roschelle, J., Knudsen, J., & Hegedus, S. "From new technological infrastructures to curricular activity systems: Advanced designs for teaching and learning." In M. J. Jacobson & P. Reimann (Eds.), *Designs for Learning Environments of the Future: International Perspectives from the Learning Sciences* (pp. 233-262). New York: Springer. 2010. Print.

Roschelle, J., Shechtman, N., Tatar, D., Hegedus, S., Hopkins, B.,

Empson, S., Knudsen, J., & Gallagher, L. "Integration of technology, curriculum, and professional development for advancing middle school mathematics: Three large-scale studies." *American Educational Research Journal*, 47(4), 833-878. 2010. Print.

Roschelle, J., Singleton, C., Sabelli, N., Pea, R., & Bransford, J. D.

"Mathematics worth knowing, resources worth growing, research worth noting: A response to the National Mathematics Advisory Panel report." *Educational Researcher*, 37(9), 610-617. 2008. Print.

Roschelle, J.,Tatar, D., Schectman, N., & Knudsen, J. "The role of scaling up research in designing for and evaluating robustness." *Educational Studies in Mathematics*, 68, 149-170. 2008. Print

Rubin, H. J. & Rubin, I. S. *Qualitative Interviewing: The Art of Hearing Data* (2nd ed.). Thousand Oaks, CA: Sage Publications. 2004. Print.

Sackett D, Richardson WS, Rosenburg W, Haynes RB. *How to Practice and Teach Evidence Based Medicine*. 2nd Ed. Churchill Livingstone. 1997. Print.

Savitt, Ronald. "Historical Research in Marketing." *Journal of Marketing* 44: 52-58. Autumn, 1980. Print.

Schütze, C. *The empirical base of linguistics: Grammaticality judgments and linguistic meth-odology.* Chicago: University of Chicago Press. 1996. Print.

Searle, J. R. "Metaphor." In: Searle, J. R.: *Expression and meaning.* Cambridge: Cambridge University Press, 76-116. 1979. Print.

Shechtman, N., Roschelle, J., Haertel, G., & Knudsen, J. "Investigating

links from teacher knowledge, to classroom practice, to student learning in the instructional system of the middle-school mathematics classroom." *Cognition and Instruction*, 28(3), 317-359. 2010. Print.

Shuttleworth, Martyn. "What is a Literature Review?" September 16, 2009. Retrieved Nov 27, 2014 from Explorable.com. https://explorable.com/what-is-a-literature-review. Web

Sims, B. R. *Technical Communication for Readers and Writers.* 2nd ed. Boston: Houghton Mifflin. 2003. Print.

Smekens Education Solutions, Inc. "Argumentative v. Persuasive Writing" http://www.smekenseducation.com/argumentative-v-persuasive-writing.html. 2015. Web. 20 January 2015.

Stake, Robert E. *The Art of Case Study Research.* Thousand Oaks, CA: SAGE, 1995. Print

Stenhouse, L. In Rudduck, J. and Hopkins, D. (eds.), *Research as a basis for teaching: readings from the work of Lawrence Stenhouse.* Oxford: Heinemann Educational. 1985. Print.

Straus S. E, Richardson W. S, Glasziou P, Haynes R. B. *Evidence Based Medicine: How to practice and teach EBM.* 3rd Ed. Elsevier Churchill Livingstone. 2005. Print.

StudyGuide.org "Film Review Guidelines." October 13, 2013. http://www.studyguide.org/fillmterms.htm. Web. 23 November 2014

Tatar, D., Roschelle, J., Knudsen, J., Shechtman, N., Kaput, J., & Hopkins, B. "Scaling up innovative technology-based math." *Journal of the Learning Sciences*, 17(2), 248-286. 2008. Print.

The Graduate Writing Center of the Center for Excellence in Writing, PSU. "Writing Thesis and Dissertation Proposals" http://pwr.la.psu.edu/resources/graduate-writing-center/handouts-1/WritingProposals.pdf/ Web. 12 January 2014

The Writing Center. University of North Carolina. "Literature Reviews." http://writingcenter.unc.edu/handouts/literature-reviews/. Web.

Wertz, F., Charmaz, K., McMullen, L., Josselson, R., Anderson, R., & McSpadden, E. *Five Ways of Doing Qualitative Research.* New York: Guilford Press. 2011. Print

"What is Literature" Basics of English Studies. (http://www2.anglistik.uni-freiburg.de/intranet/englishbasics/Home01.htm). Accessed Aug. 30, 2017. Web

Wood M. J, Ross-Kerr JC. *From question to proposal. Basic steps in planning nursing research.* 7th ed. Jones and Bartlett Publishers; 2006. Print.

Yin, Robert K. *Case Study Research: Design and Theory.* Applied Social Research Methods Series, No. 5. 3rd Ed. Thousand Oaks, CA: SAGE, 2003. Print.